Whisper
Word to the Wise

Dr. Sharon Malone Waddle

WESTBOW
PRESS®
A DIVISION OF THOMAS NELSON
& ZONDERVAN

WestBow Press books may be ordered through booksellers or by contacting:

WestBow Press
A Division of Thomas Nelson & Zondervan
1663 Liberty Drive
Bloomington, IN 47403
www.westbowpress.com
1 (866) 928-1240

Because of the dynamic nature of the Internet, any web addresses or links contained in this book may have changed since publication and may no longer be valid. The views expressed in this work are solely those of the author and do not necessarily reflect the views of the publisher, and the publisher hereby disclaims any responsibility for them.

Any people depicted in stock imagery provided by Thinkstock are models, and such images are being used for illustrative purposes only. Certain stock imagery © Thinkstock.

Cover Design Swans and Transition Photo Swans by the Author.
Red Dress Photo Credit to Mr. Benjamin Waddle.
Content Editor: Benjamin Waddle

ISBN: 978-1-5127-4704-1 (sc)
ISBN: 978-1-5127-4705-8 (hc)
ISBN: 978-1-5127-4703-4 (e)

Library of Congress Control Number: 2016910130

Print information available on the last page.

WestBow Press rev. date: 6/30/2016

Contents

Part I: Poetry

Whisper Words to the Wise by the Colonel. 1
In the Lingering 3
Reprisal of Whisper Words to the Wise 3
Lemonade 4
On the Burlap Cotton Sack. 5
Bricks and Mortar 6
It's Not God. 7
Tribute to Martha. 7
When I think about myself. 8
Tribute to Auntie 10
The Colonel's final Moment 11
If your heart was in it, we could win it (Roll up and Vote) 12
Go Zip 13
Sovereign Healing Balm 14

Part II: 2016

January Words of Whisper
Enrichment Topic: Coming Together in Unity

Introduction: What is Unity. 25
Coming Together 26
    Community Unity. 26
    In the Home. 26
    In the Workplace. 28
    In the Spirit 29
    In the Church. 29
Union with God 31
Strongholds that hinder our Union. 32
Ways to Enhance Unity. 32

Daily Preparations to ensure Unity.............................33
Summary and Conclusions.................................33

February Words of Whisper
Enrichment Topic - Agape Love
Introduction: The God Kind of Love.........................37
Types of Love 40
Practicing True Love 45
Living in Agape 46
Reaching for Love..49
Summary and Conclusions.................................50

March Words of Whisper
Enrichment Topic - Cleansing Winds
Introduction: Cleansing Winds............................53
Who is the Holy Spirit?..................................53
The Purpose for the Holy Spirit..........................58
Receiving the Promise....................................59
How to manifest the power of the Holy Spirit.............60
How to live in the Spirit 60
How to purge our sins with the help of the Spirit........61
Walking in Restoration...................................61
Summary and Conclusions.................................62

April Words of Wisdom
Enrichment Topic: The Outpouring/Showers
Introduction: Walking in the Rain 67
Preparing for Leadership: Spiritual Blessings and Spiritual Things..68
Preparing for Wealth and Health 70
The Roles of the Umbrella in the Natural and in the Spirit........71
Chasing after the Dream..................................72
Spreading Favor and Distributing Grace 73
What to do when the rain keeps pouring down 74
Summary and Conclusion 75

May Words of Wisdom
Enrichment Topic: Preparation/Graduation
Introduction: I'm Ready for the Challenge. 79
How to Plan for the Future. 79
Knowing my Assignment 80
Pursuing the Mark. 81
Persevering when the Task is Too Hard 84
Completion: Graduation Celebration Commemoration 84
Walking in Victory 85
Summary and Conclusion 85

June Words of Wisdom
Enrichment Topic: The Bridal Commitment
Introduction: The Proposal. 89
The Engagement Party. 91
Knowing How to Walk Together. 92
Accepting the Invitation 93
Walking in Sync with God 94
Commitment 94
Summary and Conclusions. 97

July Words of Wisdom
Enrichment Topic: Mission Accomplished
Walking in Purpose. 102
Staying Focused 104
Victory in Jesus Christ. 104
Summary and Conclusions. 105
Mission Impossible Ministry Skit 107

August Words of Wisdom
Enrichment Topic: New Beginnings/ Planting Season
Introduction 115
Setting Goals. 116

Planning for a Future Harvest 117
Cracking the Soil: Getting to Know you. 117
Breaking the Yoke: The Courtship. 118
Bonding: Soil and Seed 118
Commitment: Knowing how to irrigate and navigate 119
Merger: Packing /blending the soil 119
Soil, Water and Sunlight Empowerment. 120
Summary and Conclusions. 120

September Words of Wisdom
Enrichment Topic: Shekinah Glory

Introduction: The Mysteries of a Sovereign God. 123
A Peculiar People of God 124
Walking with Assurance. 125
Reaping the Harvest. 125
The Glow of His Majesty. 126
Summary and Conclusion 127

October Words of Wisdom
Enrichment Topic: Harvest Season

Introduction 131
Blessings Overflowing 132
    Exceedingly great Joy, Peace and Comfort 133
    Gathering the Harvest 133
    Plague for the Harvest 134
    Sowing on Good Ground. 135
    Who can benefit from your harvest 136
Summary and Conclusions. 137

November Words of Wisdom
Enrichment Topic – Thanksgiving

Introduction 141
The Grace and Mercy of God. 142
How to Worship God. 143

Benefits of Prayer, Praise and Worship 143
Summary and Conclusions. 144

December Words of Wisdom
Enrichment Topic: Birthing out the Promise

Introduction 147
No Cross, No Crown 147
Conception of the Spirit 149
    What you do and what you say 150
    How you react as a Christian to the promise 150
Christian Pre-Natal Care 151
Monthly Examination of Progress. 151
Pressing in on the Promise. 152
Breaking the Hymen 152
Delivery Location and Status 154
The Outpouring, Labor Pains and Deliverance. 155
Walking and living in the Promise 156
Birthing Out the Promise Summary. 157

Lessons to Learn

Ministry Lessons 161
Standard Order of Service. 162
Ministry Calendar 2017. 163
Strategic Plan for Salvation. 167
THE END 167
Key Terms and Definitions. 169
Websites. 171

Introduction

Wisdom is vital to your survival in life and is more necessary than genius intelligence and any amount of wealth. God gives wisdom freely when we ask for it, but too often we don't ask because we think our wealth, haughty profiles and ingenuity will frame our worlds and prosper us. Whisper: Word to the Wise focuses on the value of transferring vital information to the ears of an astute listener. Part I contents entail poetic messages that are insightful, inspiring and generates life changing goals, boldness and determination. Part II contents has seasonal monthly messages for Christian passageways to living a blessed life. My hopes are to connect with people who desire to listen to the voice of wisdom and have readiness to receive when God releases prevailing messages, signs and wonders. When God whispers, we must be prepared to respond quickly to receive the full benefit of his assignments. If you are listening, it's your season to receive His wisdom. Feast on this fresh manna from heaven and trust that God will whisper great and wonderful things into your lives to bring peace, phenomenal success and joy untold.

WHISPER

Part 1
Poetry

Poetry: Part 1
Whisper: Word to the Wise

Poetry: Part I

Whisper Words to the Wise by the Colonel

The colonel says a lot of wise things; she's a legend, a lady, a pepper of a thing. If you watch how she walks—with authority—you could give up all your thought. The best thing about her is she's always on the scene—bringing all the fine, traveling the horizon, and whizzing on the skyline. She's a military leader filled with might and a major contributor of education and plight. The colonel says, "Don't tell 'em nothing. Don't tell 'em nothing. And don't tell 'em nothing at all. Nothing you don't want to see in the mall, see in the hall, written on the walls. Don't tell 'em nothing at all. Don't tell 'em, cause it will be broadcast out loud, hanging on a cloud, hung on a shroud; don't tell 'em nothing at all. Don't even whisper. Don't say it low. Don't say it soft. Don't say it in the loft. *Just knock it off.* Don't tell 'em nothing at all."

The colonel says, "Don't tell nothing you don't want to see in the newspaper, written on a golf ball, pasted on the commode stall. Don't give out your all. Stand tall. Don't tell 'em nothing at all. Don't sing. Don't shout. Don't run about. Don't roar like a lion. Don't swim like a fish to bring the news. Just stop with all your might, but be sure you don't miss this: 'Don't tell 'em nothing at all.' Don't offer your good advice to a leopard with stripes, a shoe without a heel, a bird without a beak, a traitor, or a stink. Don't ramble, fuss, or scandal, just smile and think … Don't tell nothing … Don't tell 'em nothing at all."

When you get the job, hang your head and play the small. Split your paycheck and have a ball. Don't tell 'em nothing at all. Let them do what they will. Let the chips fall still. Do your best if you will. Give all you got, and still don't tell 'em nothing at all. When you're walking down the road and you see them passing by singing a song and twirling around, acting like they are having fun, nod your head and keep walking. But just don't tell 'em nothing at all.

Don't waste your prime when it's all about the time. Let em toss and turn, let 'em sting and burn, but you'd best let them learn on their own blang terms. Don't chime too soon. Don't waste your rhythm and blues. They don't want to hear your signs. Let them go in the hole and sit. Some folks got to learn in the dungeon; let them go into the pit. When they come out, all the fine. But some have to learn in their own blang time. Clang, blang, bling. Some have to do their own thing. Don't tell 'em nothing. Just sit and wait, and then celebrate when they learn on their own frame what remains. They like the blang and bling. They like to be knocked down and scream. The colonel says, "Don't tell em nothing. It's a waste of reasoning. Don't tell 'em nothing at all."

The colonel says, "I love you dearly. I salute you clearly. But really you chose not to listen. You decided not to be wise. You had to learn on your own blang time. If you have to say anything, give your words away. The Colonel says, 'Only give it to the wise.' Whisper your powerful words to the wise.

The exercise of these virtues of gentleness and a quiet spirit give us favor with God and man. Speak in the right season and for the right reason. Whisper a word to the wise.

Sincerely,
The colonel has spoken.

The mouth of the righteous speaks wisdom, and his tongue talks of justice. The law of his God is in his heart. (Psalm 37:30 –31)

Your word I have hidden in my heart, so that I might not sin against you. (Psalm 119:11 NKJV)

In Honor of Lieutenant Colonel Carolyn Rowell Culpepper-Bessemer, Alabama

In the Lingering

I bring to you good news. You turn a deaf ear and grown, my patience running thin with you. I hope it's not for long. You are malingering with my words, malingering with my thoughts, malingering with my frame of mind. If I had to malinger, I wish it would not linger, because you are malingering with my climb. My teaching time is wearing thin. I fear you will not know the lingering lessons that I hope I taught you on the go. I can't leave or say good-bye until I know that you are no longer lingering and malingering with eternity.

Reprisal of Whisper Words to the Wise

Now you wonder who Em is, and it's time to tell you. Are you ready to hear? I hope so. The colonel says Em is the baby who did not sleep at night, then becomes a teenager and wants to fuss and fight. Em is the young man who sleeps all day, the girl who never learned her way. Em is the one that makes you cry up late, sit up straight, even celebrate, but you can't tell Em nothing at all. Em is the girl that wants her hair straight, the boy that dropped his pants low, the others that don't know which way to go.

The colonel says, "You can't tell 'em nothing at all. They will soon grow up and wisdom sits in. Then they'll reach back to things you tried to put in, but for now, you can only trust your friends. Don't tell them nothing at all."

Some Ems get older and want to be *soldiers*, then fighting sets in and they run under their skin. They shut down and sigh and wish for lullaby, angry and shy and we wonder why. The pie was too hard, the crust too tough. A slither is all I'm trained to trust.

Some Ems get old and lose their souls and wonder how they could not enter in. They always wanted a way to sin; you couldn't tell em nothing at all. When the season is over and wisdom sets in, put your hand on your hip and just wink your eye. They'll soon remember and give a high five, but until nigh, you couldn't tell 'em nothing at all. The colonel has spoken, once again. "Till *nigh* you couldn't tell 'em nothing at all."

In Honor of Lieutenant Colonel Carolyn Rowell Culpepper-Bessemer, Alabama

Lemonade

Auntie says, "If you get a lemon, just make lemonade. Water it down, stir in some sugar, and serve it nice and cold." It's okay. We all make mistakes. You can turn it around. Don't wait too late. There is a point of no return. If you break your vow to water and sugar, you will have to give account. It's best to work it out. Just water it down and pour on the sugar.

I took your advice, auntie. When I had a lemon, I watered it down real good in a pretty crystal bowl, showcased, and loved on it as I was told. Made a beautiful home with all the right fixings—biscuit and butter and all the amenities. I served water, tea, and of course lemonade. Went to church and said my prayers. Did everything I thought was just and fair.

The pressure came on and the lemon went sour. Didn't know what to do from hour to hour. It's working for auntie, so surely it will work for me. It's watered down, can't you see?

I certainly poured on the water, prayed, and danced in the Holy G. Just like Maya, I think about myself and I laugh. Mercy me, Aunt Lois, I forgot the sugar.

On the Burlap Cotton Sack

In the summer after school, my siblings and I headed for the cotton field. My brothers were expected to carry the load, but the girls went for good measure. The sun was hot, the day was still long, even after school. Life has evolved and we are living a smooth life of good times and country living, kind of pleasure. Nevertheless, we have to work to press forward, so the cotton sack is not in vain. It's still here so we must continue to use it, until machinery evolves that allows us to lose it.

All it took was a creative mind to change the time. It took an inventor, a creative person with a genius mind. A person who steps out of the box at the risk of sounding odd, peculiar, and being called a dreamer. At the risk of sounding desperate to be somebody, and at the risk of being separated and alone.

My brothers pulled me on the end of the cotton sack. For me, it was game, the ride of a lifetime. To them, a distraction from the work at hand. We birth out the end of an era as we slide down the hill of segregation, poverty, needy, and lack. We didn't know much about sitting in the back. We were oblivious to the pain of transitioning; it was a natural part of life to move forward.

Past generations, my father and his siblings pulled a bale of cotton each day. Seven brothers and two sisters went on their way to meet the challenge of the day, to pay the bills and sleep four in a bed and five on the floor–and perhaps one or two with Big Mama.

Now my father's descendants pull a sack after school just to keep us off the street. So we don't think life is supposed to be too easy. My father's generation picked cotton to survive, but the next generation picked cotton to style and profile; some were just lucky to have brothers let them play and slide on the foot of the cotton sack. They picked because they were told but pulled siblings to ease the load. It's good to lose the cotton sack, but maybe we should bring it back. Surely the cotton sack has more to press us into a world of less care. The cotton sack has become extinct, but could be used for many things. The cotton sack may solve the healthcare crisis or maybe balance the national budget. We need the cotton sack to just stay black, to keep it real. We need the cotton sack hanging on the wall to remind us where we came from; we need the cotton sack to drown our tears in, we need the cotton sack to fill and punch away the cares of today. We need to frame our diplomas in burlap to represent the cotton sack, squeeze out the sap that propelled us into a land of opportunity. A little dab of sap will do, made us strong–a little sticky but we need it to thrive.

The cotton sack exposed the sky for me, taught me life is good I can be free; free to lay down and look up at a world made by a sovereign God. No one can take the sky from me; the sky is the limit is what I see laying on the foot of my brothers' cotton sacks. Whisper your cotton-picking wisdom to the wise.

Bricks and Mortar

Dad picked cotton many long years. A hard working man motivated to be independent and free. No father around to teach him anything, but many role models that he learned from all the same. Dad was a hunter; he caught many squirrels and rabbits. Mom stripped them down like a pro and cooked them like filet Mignon–at least that's what it seem like when dad ate them. A delicacy from the hands of a self-made man. He put it all together and always had a plan, always ready and prepared. He made life look easy. He paid cash for everything. Tried to get a loan and couldn't sleep all night went to the bank the next day and paid them off … It's a load he did not want to carry. The house payment was 52.00 a month but he soon paid it off. Laughing all the way home.

He built homes and finished them with brick; a designers' original. My brothers labored with dad on Saturdays to mix and carry the mortar. They are all designers' original. Work never hurt anyone, whispered from the brick to the mortar.

Mom a Nurse and dad a Brick Mason, made a Psychologist, a Psalmist and Author. A little work never hurt anyone, whispered from the brick to the mortar.

It's Not God

You could get with her but it would not be God. It's not a match made in heaven. It would not be smooth. You could get with him but the whistles won't blow the bells won't ring, it would be just a flesh type thing. When she's the right one, Shekinah Glory will come and retreat in the temple. When it's God it will be smooth, it will reach into his soul.

You could get with her, but it would not be God. It's too complicated and feels kinda odd. She could get with you but the road would be rough, it could just be a charismatic situation, later the elevator will drop. He could get with, her but it would not be God—It would not satisfy your thirst, I'm not who you were born to serve. You are not the one to help me with my pride. I could get with you, but it would not be God. I could get with you but, the journey would not be good. Make sure it's a match made by God. Praise God!

Tribute to Martha

Martha says I'm precious, who else would even know. It must be Jesus, who had to tell her, don't you know? Days we felt unworthy, but she spoke with a surety; "You are so very precious, you mean the world to me".

Martha is a pearl recessed in the hands of God. Martha was called out because she is His chosen one. God opened the shell so we could see your beauty; closed it, then reached from heaven, so we would know His love.

You are God's daughter Martha; He never let you go. You were crushed to make us strong; He embraced you to teach us to trust him. He has done great and marvelous things in you. You have built a sanctuary in your heart for God's people. A place of refuge, that will forever live on; a home we can always know. There is no mansion to compare to your love. Nothing could separate us from your love. Your love will move mountains and flow through valleys into the crevices of despair, but then, we reflect on the power of your love. We gain strength at the thought of you. You are a woman of God, teaching with patience, gentleness, so sweet and kind, God's' angel sent from heaven. You are the precious treasured one. You lived a precious life and made precious sacrifices to love everyone and encouraged the children, leaving a legacy for generations to come.

God whispered words of peace in you Martha; we experienced your harmony with God. Martha overlooked our faults and believed that we were worthy of high praise and exaltation, just as she continually praised God through the storms. What an honor to know you; you were so easy to love. God's precious Pearl–the chosen one. We will do great things because of what you saw and believed in us. You sustained us, blessed us and set us free. We salute you Martha because you are the precious one–a lady of God indeed.

Precious memories from the family, In memory of Martha Rice, RIP 2014

When I think about myself

When I think about myself, I see a lady filled with energy and plans, walking in a fervent stand. Too serious to comprehend, when she thinks about herself. She see a young girl playing in a simple world, trying to smile and twirl doing everything in sync, when she thinks. When she think about the scholar, working hard to make a dollar, she see steadfast and overcoming, loading up on power when she think about herself. A no non-sense kind of girl. Silly days and loving nights, pushing forward against the resistance, don't know to back off and let it flow, pushing harder, when she thinks. She's often laughing, playing, entertaining in style, oblivious to the snares and cares. Absolutely you can depend, pressing in understand, giving all and more, choking out the nays and noers, she don't relent, pressing down to the core, she stretch, bless and rest.

When she thinks about herself, she can weather any storm, holding on to Father and Son. Life has been rugged and smooth; Dancing and singing, strolling with the enemy and rocking with the challenges of each new day. It's been interesting to say the least, but God has lifted her in comfort and peace. She still rises above the cloud, gently praising the Lord out loud, celebrated by none and yet, she still rise.

Never taking time to breathe–always moving forward in deed. Going from day to day, making life endurable, usable, functional, delectable, complexity on wheels –yet steel. Flipping in the sand, blessings on demand, sharing and caring, giving and forgiving on a platter.

Tender and pleasant sometimes intense and gently sweet, unique-when she thinks. Singing with a melody way out in the horizon, anointed and passionate, graced with a smooth tongue, the feelings internal makes me hum a song. Solid friend, convicted and tolerant, yet strong and determined. Righteous persistence, giving every opportunity for others to shine, patiently waiting and then she unwinds. Waited too long, but the roots grew deep, power inside---she don't sink. Plowing the mule despite the tricks and games, going forward just the same. Whisper it softly—transformed and few, illuminating the darkest places, with wisdom and truth. Word to the Wise ...

Tribute to Auntie

Auntie is the most consistent person that I know. She does not quiver with circumstances and situations. She is a country girl with elegance and grace. She is unassumingly beautiful and so unselfish that, she does not know that she is a Queen. She does not focus on beauty or style because, it focuses on her. Beauty beckons her to come into its presence– she does not take two steps to find it. Beauty finds her and takes a bow at her existence. She is the same yesterday, today and is estimated to be the same forevermore.

Auntie is balanced during any personality of a day. She is forthright and does not relent. She will tell any beast or man, "I don't bite my tongue". What you see is what it is. She looks you straight in the eye – no sorrow, no pain, no shame. She is humble and wise, uneasily tricked or fooled. She defeats effortlessly and with endearment. She is brave and unafraid of any challenge that life brings forth. She exuberates love, wellbeing and security for the family. She's everyone's girl, she shows up and transforms our world. She does her best and has no apologies to make. She is sincere.

Auntie is a Godly woman, she belongs to the King. She has kind words and she whispers softly to the wise. She does not waste time with anyone who does not appreciate her company. She saves her virtue for ones who can receive at the most opportune moment in time. She taught us to turn our heads and blow back at the wind. When hot air comes forth, give it no importance – blow it away.

When winds of confusion comes, dust it off, regroup, smile and let it settle in the elements, lift it to the heavens, consume it in the sky, whisper gently good bye. It has its' place up high. Blow it in the wind.

Thank you for all the things you taught to build our character. Thank you for being available to share your gifts with every generation and thanks so much for the good food, cakes, pies and your culinary gifts over the years. You will always be a joy to my eyes. Much love aunties!

Your Niece Always,
-Dr. Sharon Malone Waddle

The Colonel's final Moment

At the end of the story, the colonel becomes aloft. She has her retainers make a grocery list and her aid cleans up the house. Decorated with honor a soldier to the core, she stand firm in position and goes straight to deploy. She sends the butler shopping and calls a party planner to celebrate the crew. She invites the whole team from the oldest to the new. She gets music and gifts and fruit I'm told. She gives out awards and scholarships for the young sirs and all of the misses. She tells them when you finish college, I have an endowment waiting very soon or I would be remiss. Even for the ones writing in the elevator, walking down the escalator that she could tell nothing. Even for the ones who pushed her buttons, skipped school, tried to be cool, played game, didn't know her name, stole out of her purse, was seen in her limousine, tried to put her in a hearse. Forgiveness is still clean, fashionable and in style, on the scene.

Positive rewards always come through when someone hears the whispered words meant for you. Whisper a word to the wise. Whisper your precious word to the upcoming, mobile, sane and true. Blessings always come to the wise and faithful. The colonel says, "Trust God and do Good". The colonel speaks words of wisdom to those with an ear inclined to hear. The colonel commands attention from the rulers of this land–If you were not included, don't you understand? She will not waste time for the fickle or the slouch, get prepared if it takes you out your comfort zone, saddle up and go the distance prepare to reign even if you have to go alone. If the Colonel tries to speak, stand in attention and hear it all, the Colonel paid a price to declare, so listen and stop the brawl. I said, "Listen to it all". The Colonel whispers a word to the wise, the legacy remains. The Colonel Exits.

Whew! Psalms 27: 13 "I would have fainted unless I believed in the goodness of God in the land of the living".

In honor of Lieutenant Colonel, Carolyn Rowell Culpepper-Bessemer, Alabama

If your heart was in it, we could win it (Roll up and Vote)

It's time to roll up at the polls and vote. Set your alarm to rush in and take authority. Election time has come again and now we know it's time to bend and place the card into the slot, it's got to count or make a shot, your seed–it really means a lot. My heart has groaned with pass miscounts, I have to send my own shout out. My heart has grown and now I need to tell the world it's just a seed to meet a need. If you plant your seed in the election box, it's sure to raise the options out.

If your heart was in it, we could win. If your heart was in it we could bless the land. Your heart has to know to tow the road, because it must be in so we can win. You get your heart in by checking the news, your heart has to know all the feuds, so to make a difference the heart must see a ballot coming to help poll the vote, set the table and plan for the able. We all can benefit when we share in the feast, bring your best options, and water your seed to meet the need.

We can all win if we put in our best thoughts, sift all the evil out and walk about to water the best candidates based on the mandates; planning for the sunny days hovering in the amazing ways . We are obligated to follow order when we want our seeds to fix the edict we must be about the veto, so we can share in the egos of winners and champions for the people. The law decrees, where we should be, if we fail to vote, we fail to see the places where we desire to abide and thrive. If your heart was in it we could win it.

If your heart was in it we could win it. If your heart was in it we could win it. If your heart was in it we could win it. If your heart was in it we could win it. We could pull down the instigators messing up the legislators. Roll up and roll up. We can satisfy the population, orchestrate the immigration. Roll up and roll up. We can manage the healthcare needs and sift out the ill by voting all you got with a plan to fit the bill with the right candidate in the palm of your hand. Roll up. Roll up and vote. If your heart was in it we could win it. If your heart was in it we could win it. If your heart was in it we could win it. If your heart was in it we could win it. We could pull down the instigators sabotaging the legislators. Roll up and roll up. We can satisfy the population, orchestrate the immigration Roll up and roll up. We can manage the healthcare needs and sift out the ill by voting all you got with a plan to fit the bill with the right candidate in the palm of your hand. Roll up and roll up and vote.

Roll up: Whisper Word to the Wise

Go Zip

We use to hide the zipper and close it in a case. The zipper does a lot for us but sometimes makes us late. The zip can sometimes come off track at the most inconvenient time. It's such an unfortunate thing, and just a waste of time. You can't repair a zipper, unless you cut it in the crack and if you don't sew it up it falls off just like that. You can slide it down a little, but if you cross the line, the zipper that you need will crash and lose its kind.

A snap will often help you, but sometimes it pops right off. Some snaps last forever, but we cannot be soft. A loop is sometimes helpful if the latch stays fluff and strong, but not sure it stays in place, it may twist off with your turn at cost and at your loss.

Excuse me, I need to go zip a bit; I'm not striving with you, you can zip or flip; I'm trying to choose if I should rip or sip. Everyone loses when you rip a zip; you can't get it back, you must dispose, just like nylon hose, when you rip it's a rap that never zaps back. Sipping sometimes relaxes the zip and loosens the lip. Slip out for elastic, or maybe something more drastic; Pull it over your head is what someone said, but the zip is more hip, I would rather go flip back for my zip.

The zip stands outside, no longer tries to hide. The new zip is proud and sings out loud. Look at me I'm moving forward in scene. I'm bright and bedazzling, it's my season to bling. You can find me on the dress front and back, on your slacks, ripping up and down the legs, in the peg on the elbow just for show, you better go zip if you want to be in style in 2014. Go zip on my boots, on my socks, on my headband, gloves and on the locks, every day you can zip it off. Whatever you care about, rest at the table, make sure you're able, just zip it off. Go zip. Word to the wise. Just go zip.

You can zip your mouth, stop showing it off, it gets you in trouble, move you backwards and forwards. Stay consistent and true just zip it off. Go zip it close, so it no longer holds your future. Go zip for my sake. Go zip.

Sovereign Healing Balm

Voice: Be strong and courageous.

Lead: Be strong and courageous. Move forward like a breeze. God is healer and reaches down to heal my needs. Be vigilant and steadfast, walk confident and sure, my God is healer and mends wounds we cannot see. God flows through my body and cleans the deep hurt and pain. He releases the trap and life flows like a refreshing morning spring. He moves like the wind and heals like the rain. He comes in with power and deletes the hidden things. Things that hinder and block my healing, He takes it all away. Things that slow you down, God heals like He's the Sovereign King. He keeps his promises, trust him to birth healing out on every opportunity.

Chorus: He's a healing balm. He's a healing balm. He's the only one. He's a healing balm. Master, you're the only one. Stay with me God, stay with me now, don't leave me, I need your help to fly. I desire to soar. Oh Lord I need you now. Brighten my days, fill me with worship and praise. Oh Lord I need you now. My healing balm. Truth be told, I need you to heal me with your healing balm. Come Lord, come now. Heal the nation. Let your kingdom come. You are my sovereign healing balm.

Lead: Move forward trust in Jehovah, Sovereign God and risen King. Storms come to test our faith, melodies come to make us sing. We sing holy, holy, great Redeemer, Pastor me as the choir sings. You are my Sovereign Savior, I surrender my life and praise with patience forever. I'm committed to you alone. Heal me with your healing balm.

Lead: Saturate me with your presence, massage me with your love and peace, I long for you Messiah, I need your power to breathe. Touch me now Lord great Redeemer, Hosanna teach me how to love. Show me how to whisper healing, teach me to whisper wisdom and help me whisper words of love. Make me fertile for the harvest, shape me through the wind and rain. Fill me with your presence…then breathe life in me once again.

Chorus: He's a healing balm. He's a healing balm. He's the only one. He's a healing balm. Master, you're the only one. Stay with me God, stay with me now, don't leave me, I need your help to fly. I desire to soar. Oh Lord I need you now. Brighten my days, fill me with worship and praise. Oh Lord I need you now. My healing balm. Truth be told, I need you to heal me with your healing balm. Come Lord, come now. Heal the nation. Let your kingdom come. You are my sovereign healing balm.

Lead: I can press on, I can weather the storm because you lift me up. You sanctify, glorify and edify your chosen ones. Manifest now, healing as I sing, bring your mighty power blowing healing, moving healing on everything as I walk, talk and breathe. Anointing me with healing power, teach me everything.

Chorus 1: He's a healing balm. He's a healing balm. He's the only one. He's a healing balm. Master, you're the only one. Stay with me God, stay with me now, don't leave me, I need your help to fly. I desire to soar. Oh Lord I need you now. Brighten my days, fill me with worship and praise. Oh Lord I need you now. My healing balm. Truth be told, I need you to heal me with your healing balm. Come Lord, come now. Heal the nation. Let your kingdom come. You are my sovereign healing balm.

Chorus 2: Let your balm in Gilead heal my soul. Oh God, please let your balm in Gilead heal my soul. Take me to the Jordan River and Oh God, please anoint me with the saving grace of Gilead, from the mountain of Jordan River–your healing balm. Truth be told, I need your healing balm. Thank you Lord…for your healing balm.

Voice: Be strong and courageous. Jeremiah 8:22 speaks loudly to my soul, "Is there no balm in Gilead? Is there no Physician there? Why then is there no healing for the wound of my people? My sins are buried in the Jordan River.

Choir voice: I am strong and courageous. I surrender. Bring the ultimate power of your healing balm from the mountains of the Jordan River heal my soul. The wounds are no longer in my soul. Your love smells like evergreen on my soul. Amen

Lead: Let me smell the fragrance of healing deep in the residue of wounds no longer in my soul. Your love smells like evergreen in my soul. Thank you Lord for trusting me with the power of your healing balm. Thank you for sanctifying me, thank you purging me, thank you for being Lord of Lord's and King of Kings. Thank you for being Jehovah Rophe', the greatest healer that ever was and ever will be. Wonderful God everlasting healer, Redeemer, Savior of the world. I smell the fragrance of healing deep in the residue of wounds no longer in my soul. Your love smells like evergreen in my soul. Thank you Lord for trusting me with the power of your healing balm.

Chorus: He's a healing balm. He's a healing balm. He's the only one. He's a healing balm. Master, you're the only one. Stay with me God, stay with me now, don't leave me, I need your help to fly. I desire to soar. Oh Lord I need you now. Brighten my days, fill me with worship and praise. Oh Lord I need you now. My healing balm. Truth be told, I need you to heal me with your healing balm. Come Lord, come now. Heal the nation. Let your kingdom come. You are my sovereign healing balm.

Chorus: He's a healing balm. He's a healing balm. He's the only one. He's a healing balm. Master, you're the only one. Stay with me God, stay with me now, don't leave me, I need your help to fly. I desire to soar. Oh Lord I need you now. Brighten my days, fill me with worship and praise. Oh Lord I need you now. My healing balm. Truth be told, I need you to heal me with your healing balm. Come Lord, come now. Heal the nation. Let your kingdom come.

Lead: Bless the Lord, Oh my soul and all that is within me praise his holy name. Nothing will separate me from the love of God. God is my rock and my fortress. He is a very present help in the times of all my trouble. In my despair, I called upon the name of the Lord and he rescued me from all my trouble. His healing balm is smoother than ice, his healing balm is more-gentle than a cool breeze, and his ointment has a fragrance more lovely, than fine silk cloth. Taste and see that his healing is good. Only you Lord, master only you can heal the nation. Proclaim your healing balm rolls over the nations. Master, Master, Good Master when you say it, it is done. When you speak healing it comes to past. You are the wonderworking majestic healer. You are savior of the world. You feed the hungry, give shelter to the poor. You are our rock and our fortress. A very present help in the storm. Most high God, most high God, the greatest Physician. Saturate us with your healing balm.

> Chorus: He's a healing balm. He's a healing balm. He's the only one. He's a healing balm. Master, you're the only one. Stay with me God, stay with me now, don't leave me, I need your help to fly. I desire to soar. Oh Lord I need you now. Brighten my days, fill me with worship and praise. Oh Lord I need you now. My healing balm. Truth be told, I need you to heal me with your healing balm. Come Lord, come now. Heal the nation. Let your kingdom come. You are my sovereign healing balm.

Voice: Be strong and courageous. Jeremiah 8:22 speaks loudly to my soul, "Is there no balm in Gilead? Is there no Physician there? Why then is there no healing for the wound of my people? My sins are buried in the Jordan River.

Choir voice: I am strong and courageous. I surrender. Bring the ultimate power of your healing balm from the mountains of the Jordan River heal my soul. The wounds are no longer in my soul. Your love smells like evergreen on my soul. You are my sovereign healing balm. Amen

> Chorus: He's a healing balm. He's a healing balm. He's the only one. He's a healing balm. Master, you're the only one. Stay with me God, stay with me now, don't leave me, I need your help to fly.

I desire to soar. Oh Lord I need you now. Brighten my days, fill me with worship and praise. Oh Lord I need you now. My healing balm. Truth be told, I need you to heal me with your healing balm. Come Lord, come now. Heal the nation. Let your kingdom come. I'm healed… with your sovereign healing balm.

Written by Dr. Sharon Malone Waddle
Composed by Dr. Michael Hambrick

WHISPER MINISTRY LESSONS

Part II
2016

Whisper: Word to the Wise

Vignettes I:
January Words of Whisper
Enrichment Topic: Coming Together in Unity

Vignette 1

Coming Together in Unity
Vignettes 1: January Words of Whisper

Coming Together in Unity

Introduction: What is Unity

In union there is harmony and a beat of rhythm that allows the soul to be at peace. January is the month to refresh and step forward with exhilaration and readiness. Unity is having a mind that embraces everyone. Unity stands for togetherness and a lack of separation or an absence of schism. Unity implies we, us, our and everyone. It's time to think about how much we use these terms and make effort to increase the number of times from week to week henceforth. It is time to reduce the number of times we say," I, me, mine and myself". We must approach life in reference to what has value for humans collectively. What is going to allow us to get the results that we favor? We are starting with a blank slate, we can press the refresh button on the functions of our memory, deleting things from the past to pave a path that will move all of us towards a higher level of cohesion to manifest greater success. Last year was wonderful; however, this year and the years hereafter will be greater because we walk in harmony.

Now, because we walk together, we annihilate poverty, sickness, pain, disease, lack, ambivalence, hatred, strife and indifference. Unity will allow us to delete mortgage balances, student loans, Healthcare bills, airplane fees and fees from hotel accommodations. All of these issues have hindered our pleasures in life. Without these road blocks, we could travel the world over and return to our homes and workplace with enjoyment, enthusiasm and vigor. So we have opted to refresh, we are brand new and we are smelling like a fresh rose of opportunity. We are no longer contaminated, aggravated, frustrated because we are now walking in the promise. We cleared out every weighted burden and will not recall any of the pain again. "This is the day that the Lord has made ... We will rejoice and be glad in it", is what my Uncle always says before he ministers. Whisper these words to the wise, because only the wise can comprehend and celebrate a new day to rest in Jesus. Ecclesiastes 9:17 (NIRV) "People should listen to the quiet words of those who are wise.

Coming Together

Community Unity

Unity is vital in the community because everyone benefits when they can sleep well and awaken rejuvenated. When we can trust our neighbors to look out for us, it gives us confidence and assurance to turn the lights off and rest in Jesus. Lack of unity in the neighborhood would make everyone wired, tense, uptight, rude and restless. Sometimes friends tell me to get a security system and I tell them, my neighbors are my security. We are on one accord and the ones with a security camera are close enough to cover my house, is what I jokingly tell them. In my heart there is a hope and belief that we are all covered by the blood of Jesus, by our faithfulness and by the words of our testimony. We press the refresh button every day and we expect deliverance from every attack from the enemy.

In the Home

In the home, family members should use every gift available to benefit everyone collectively. Working together, considering the needs of each other and using the best skill, talent and ability that each person has to offer. God put each person there to contribute something that will press everyone towards a closer relationship with Him. When families operate in love and respect for each other, the home has a sweet aroma. The atmosphere is inviting and the blessings of God overflow so that their household is blessed to be a blessing to extended family, neighbors and friends. Without harmony, chaos creeps into the gaps. Parents are the head of the household and set the atmosphere for what happens to everyone. The husband is responsible for everything that goes right or wrong. Too often, we as parents spend time beating down the children, when we should evaluate what gave the youth the idea that what they did was acceptable. Where is the missing link, how did drugs get in the gap? Where did the gap come from and how long has it been lingering and invading. Sometimes, we need to hold up and be quiet, assess what we do and how we operate as parents. Too often we are out shopping, leaving a gap; getting our hair and nails done, leaving a gap; talking on the telephone, leaving a gap; and doing everything but making certain that we hear the gentle groans and discontent in the eyes of our children. Your husbands are whispering, but we are not wise enough to hear. Your children are sighing but we do not hear. This is the season to hear the gentle whispers and whisper back words to the wise. Children are teachable if we stay on course, make them important and they will reciprocate, because you taught then well to value people. Husbands and wives are married for a reason; therefore, we need to talk and listen, to find exactly where the breakdown developed. I counseled with a friend and told him, "you are not listening—you are so busy talking, stop to listen to your wife. Let there be silence for as long as it takes for your spouse to speak again and continue listening. Let her speak 3-4 times before you say a word. Just pay attention and listen. It does not matter if the silence becomes uncomfortable, wait and listen some more. This is too critical to miss -- what is she saying?" We are so fixated on what we said that we often don't really hear the heart of what others are communicating. So we are charged to listen more and talk less. We are on the brink of breakthrough and the key is our ability to listen. Once the full revelation manifest, we can then whisper back with power and authority to regain unity for the lost moments. Speaking too quickly we miss everything needed to recover. There is a point of no return. How well you listen is key to successful family unity.

The least of the least often have the most important things to say. The words of the wise, presented by the new employee are often overlooked and deemed of no importance. Ten years later, the system of authority finally decides to embrace what was said years prior, but they could not receive it from the least senior person. Failure to listen created a budget crisis. The new comers role is to bring a fresh perspective; however, there is a tendency to suffocate and snuff out good advice whispered from the wise and upwardly mobile. Because the senior staff are motivated by reaching for retirement, they may not be driven to venture into new endeavors that are the zeitgeist (spirit of the times) movement. A critical point where urgency is necessary, but everyone sits down and spin with no effort towards making timely decisions. Unity is so important and thinking towards the future is necessary to prepare for the next generation of workers. I'm working myself out of a job because I want the next generation to come in and do greater things, to press me into my destiny beyond the workplace. I'm ready to get on board because what I learn from the newcomers is seed for my next job, even if the next job is retirement. I want to be in sync so much that my mind is organized and prepared to enjoy the fullest blessings of my retirement season. What we learn in the workplace should carry over into household efficiency and organization. Being united in the workplace, helps us to work in unison at home, at church, on vacation and where ever we are led to go for representation. The next generation needs liberty to spread their wings, while they are young; because they can feed the workplace system twice as fast and teach us all greater levels of efficiency. They are typically willing to put the time in, if we are unselfish enough to allow them to soar. Their purpose is to ease the load, but we often load them down with our antiquated methods. We battle against the blessings that God sent to make us free. When new people come, they have fresh sap that will flow like rivers if we don't plug off the source. Their brains are energized and flowing with witty ideas and inventions, if we would embrace them and get onboard.

In the Spirit

As Christian, we should be so connected that our instincts tell us when something is wrong or when people are operating out of character. Instead of thinking she is stuck up, maybe we should think, "She needs a genuine friend to talk to". We also have to recognize when we are not the person to console or talk to them. It's important to designate or solicit someone to talk, who can make a difference for a specific person. Sure, I know you think you are the one, but if history has not worked in the past, or if there is a bad vibe, then you are not the one for this moment. One day it occurred to me that a friend had not called for longer than usual, so I just sent him a text message, "R U O K?" He said, "Why do you ask Sharon?" I knew by his response that something was not okay. He could have said yes or no, but he was amazed that I asked, because he was at a low moment and had spoken to no one. I told him, "I feel your heart". If someone mows the yard for three hours of course they need a break, water, air or some type of refreshment. A Good Samaritan would offer water. Nothing spiritual about that- just good looking out. However, when you can feel the heart of someone across town, next door, in New York, Hawaii, South Korea and reach out to that person, you are walking in the power of God- that's how Christians should operate.

In the Church

The church has an opportunity to regain a reputation for oneness and union. January is a great time to set a standard that may have slipped or been neglected. As a church member we must know that we are not in competition, but we are to be in fellowship. Old ideas are going to get old antiquated results. Too often the young generation is pressed down until their fire burns out. The older generation are holding on to positions and taking no moments to train the next generation to get better prepared. The church becomes stagnant because older adults are competing with young folks and not embracing the creativity that God placed in their hearts. The love must be so strong that we see the gifts of God in the youth. If we want them to be millionaires tithing in the church we need to give them the value early on that they are important and necessary. If you are 65 or over someone 25 should be doing your job and you should be mentoring. If you have been the church secretary for 20 years, you should be training someone else with a business degree to play the role that you have played and empower them to do an even greater job than yourself. You are still of great value; you are still very important to the body, but if you hold the position until you die, no one can benefit from your skills, knowledge and ability. Thus the church never grows, it remains small. The leadership in the church must be refreshed and empowered to go higher. The church waits too long to empower the youth, so the youth seek the world to anoint them. The church blames parents and neighbors and friends for destroying the youth, but the church destroys the youth by not recognizing their gifts early and appointing them to stations in church business that give them importance and direction. The talent that could have remained at the home church has to find its' way to a congregation that is not jealous and pressing down the God given gifts. Unfortunately, many times the youth are so discouraged that the gifts never make it back to any church. We had them and we pushed them away. The Church is responsible for the lost youth; we never embraced them, we never let them soar; we pressed our thumbs down on them and made them tuck their heads down and drown in our outdated methods. Nevertheless, the good news is that we are still alive and able to get it right. Now, we are charged to let the youth run the church and give them the tools they need to make it work. We are now empowered to prosper for generations to come. Make them deacons at age 18 while they are teachable and seeking to know who they are and what their roles in life are supposed to be. The ones 14 will be watching and encouraged that they only have 4 years to anticipate the same blessing. Appoint the young ladies to the board of mothers to attest to their womanhood by age 18. By age 40 they have gotten too distracted by the world—they needed an early affirmation to get them stable and mature. We blew it, sitting in the church. Let's embrace the youth while they are energetic and ready. Unison will be pleasing to the Lord and we will see strong young families evolve in the church. They will be sustained by your blessings and honor.

Union with God

We know that we are in harmony with God, when we prosper in our minds, body and souls. We must eat nutritious meals to hear from God; we must think things that are lovely, true and of good report to hear from God and our souls must be rested, to know that God is sovereign and fully equipped to meet our every need. We need to teach the children early that God takes care of his children, when his sons and daughters rest and trust Him. Teenagers are worried about bills and concerned that they will be embarrassed if they don't have the luxuries that the rich and famous celebrities enjoy. We did not empower them to rest in Jesus. Perfect harmony with God allows us to build our faith in God to meet our needs and desires. God says he will give us the desires of our hearts. We must teach youth to go into their closets to honor God, develop a personal relation-ship with God early, so we can delete the years that the enemy steals. Training the youth early to be blessed all their years will position them to have those desires in the perfect time of God. Union with God allows us to be glad at every moment. Union with God makes us complete and renews our youth. Even now as older adults and seniors if we don't already have the revelation, we must spend some time to allow it to enter into our hearts and minds. God loves you and he will provide, when we trust him and rest. We cannot dishonor God by planning and scheming to get things, positions and wealth. Wait patiently and God will blow your minds with things, positions, places, salaries and soul mates beyond your wildest imagination. All the things nor money have power to bring joy long-term. People are most important. When we love God's people and desire to be a blessing, then he allows us have the wealth and health to be leaders and advocates for his beloved. Unity with God requires that we love man and only allow the joy of the Lord to rest on your minds.

Strongholds that hinder our Union

Negative thoughts and outlooks are tools used by the enemy to stagnate us and keep us going in a cycle of lack and just enough. We have to be consistently positive in our minds and in our outlooks to gain good results. Failure to focus on positive things will end up with negative results. The scripture says that we will get those things that we are expecting and our expectations will not be denied or cut off. Proverbs 23: 17-19 (NASB) "Do not let your heart envy sinners, but live in the fear of the LORD always. Surely there is a future, and your hope will not be cut off. Listen, my son, and be wise, and direct your heart in the way." This compels us to look for the good 24/7. Because good is what we need to survive and thrive in the Kingdom of God.

Ways to Enhance Unity

Prayer, Praise and Worship beckons unity, peace and harmony in our lives. The prayer of the righteous avails much. We need much, so we must pray, petition our thanksgiving to the Lord so He manifest his storehouse of riches, blessings and honor. Love must always be added to the equation to live a Christ like lifestyle. Love never fails. Prayer is a method to join forces with the power of God to gain access to the kingdom of God. Prayer is a lifestyle to show that we acknowledge that we need God to team up with us, to make greatness known in us in the earth. Praise shows that we honor Him for staying in the battle with us and is a means to show our witness to his promises. Worship expresses our surrender that we trust God to do it all alone. We worship because the struggle is all on God. Isaiah 49:15 says, "Can a woman forget her nursing child, that she should not have compassion on the son of her womb? Yea, they may forget, yet will I not forget thee".

God takes our cares, our sins and made them vanish, so we are sold, by way of the love of God, whereas he cuts through the clouds and pours out his care and blessings to sustain us. The same way a mother cares for her children, likewise, God never forgets us. He is always on standby to make provisions for our lives. We praise and partner with God because he does all the work, treats us like royalty and let us take credit for good results. Who would not sign a contract with a sovereign God? He is all knowing, all caring, all and all, through it all. Commune with God, He gives us perfect leverage to win every battle.

Daily Preparations to ensure Unity

Be determined each day to stay balanced and not be moved by unexpected events. Talk to God throughout the day to build up your confidence and knowledge that nothing will be too hard as long as He is with you. Take Him with you everywhere you go and all challenges will seem so small. Make melody in your heart. Sing a love song to God and He will stay with you to hear it all day long. Play a love song on your media choice if you don't sing or hum. Even God can't resist a love song. He will keep you in perfect peace, as you shower him with love and let love infuse the environment.

Summary and Conclusions

My purpose is to prosper you, by whispering a word to the wise. We are all ready for change that turns around every bad situation, so we must change our posture, change our mind set and look for the good in every event. Your expectation will live and grow as you breathe in the breath of life. Smell the aroma of God in every project or vision that you perceive. His aroma will bring you into your wealthy place; His touch will revive every dead situation; His voice will rearrange, prosper and elevate you. Bring his brand of fragrance into your world. Forget those things behind and press towards a prosperous invigorating today and tomorrow. I am so honored that you are listening and learning to whisper a timely word to the wise. I am so blessed that you can only speak at the right season and for the right reason. Thank you for listening to the hearts and groans of your co-workers, pew members of the church, associates and friends. God in his infinite wisdom will use us all to prosper each person. Don't count me out, I'm a willing vessel for Christ. Let the joy of the Lord sustain your strength, your peace and your love. Let love be your weapon at all times and perfect unity will flourish you and embellish you with the victorious salvation and overcoming power of God.

References: Coming Together in Unity

Psalms 133:1 (AKJV) Behold, how good and how pleasant it is for brothers to dwell together in unity!

Whisper: Word to the Wise

Vignettes II:
February Words of Whisper
Enrichment Topic - Agape Love

Vignette II Agape Love

Introduction: The God Kind of Love

Love is whispered in so many ways and platforms. A simple "Hello" or smile are measures of love at the start of a new day. Love manifest when we first see our parents and siblings entering into a new world. Love happens when we meet the person that we want to date and ultimately marry. Love is expressed when we conceive and celebrate the birth of a new born baby; love is expressed when we give allowances to our children for good grades. Love is expressed upon graduation day, when we are showered with so many gifts and surprises. Life is filled with opportunities to love and be the warm and joyful persons that God designed us to be. Bottles, teething rings and pacifiers were an initial expression of love that transforms into greater things in life that gives us comfort. Playgrounds, amusement parks and venues to ride and cycle, later play grand roles in our observations of love. Simple pleasures in life swells up feelings of love and well-being. Sharing an ice cream cone with a favorite friend or buddy is a love that cannot be explained, except it makes you feel delight. Love is displayed sitting on the grounds at a college campus and waiting for band rehearsal to pass by with entertainment. Love is landing one's first job and getting paid; using your own money to do things that bring enjoy. Love is buying or receiving the first strand of pearls for a wedding present or unexpected Gatorade on a sunny and humid day.

It's in our best interest to think the best, so why do we fight against our own-selves. I have been expecting the worst from people since childhood and often I got the worst and exceedingly more – pressed down shaken together and running over. I am now in the process of renewing my mind to expect the best, because I'm tired of the good, bad and the ugly. I want consistently the best love.

1 Corinthians 13:4-8 (NIV)

Verse [4] Love is patient, love is kind. It does not envy, it does not boast, it is not proud. Verse[5] It does not dishonor others, it is not self-seeking, it is not easily angered, it keeps no record of wrongs. Verse [6] Love does not delight in evil but rejoices with the truth. Verse [7] It always protects, always trusts, always hopes, and always perseveres. Verse[8] Love never fails. But where there are prophecies, they will cease; where there are tongues, they will be stilled; where there is knowledge, it will pass away. To bond and develop relationships that are pleasing to God, we must humble ourselves and not think too highly of ourselves. Often we point the finger at others, but fail to evaluate our own shortcomings. When we make business transaction we want the vendor to show love and favor to us, but we also need to show love and favor to our own customers in like manner. Whoever you serve deserves the same protection and honor. I can't give a better deal to this customer anticipating that they can perform an equal favor in another venue. Love says this is fair and just and I'm willing to do this for anyone. Sure we make concessions when someone obviously cannot afford our product; but we need to be alert regarding elevating prices because we think someone else can afford to pay more.

When we have a heart of love, we can wait, we can be patient and give the vendor an opportunity to do the right thing. In traffic we can humor the person weaving through traffic by deferring at the thought of blowing our horns and allowing them the honor to move ahead. As Christians we have to make a conscious effort to cancel out the wrong of others by deleting it from memory, by assuming that they have some urgent need to do what they did and by praying a prayer that they will rest and trust God to take care of that anxious behavior that manifest in their deeds, words and posture. We are charged to keep no record of wrong. Don't count the number of times she bumped against you in a crowd; be honored that she did not feel too good to touch or be touched. Make a moment of love.

Sometimes we try to bow guard people who appear to be rude. Most of the time it's best to take a bow and let them move forward without any risk of collision. Too often, we boast that "I would not let her pass me or I taught him a thing". Instead, we just need to whisper "good-bye, keep it moving sir/mam". Pride comes right before we fall—and a haughty spirit before destruction. Immediately before we self-destruct with our wicked decisions to block and barricade others, we became too self-righteous, too arrogant.

When we first meet new friends, we are patient and kind, but over time we become too familiar and risk damaging the love by saying and doing things that weakens the bond and confidence that has been established. People want love to be strong and consistent. We need people to accept us where we are and build us up so that we can reach the next platform effortlessly. Love has to believe that God is hearing your whispered prayers and He is transforming that friend to be all that He desires them to be. Too often we want the perfect friend or soul mate; however, sometimes God puts us with people who can scrape the rust off of us and help us to become smooth and better tools, useful to build up his kingdom.

We need to be willing to protect others who do not consider our needs. We say we want to be the head and not the tail, but are we willing to speak words of love and esteem to those who degrade us and say all manner of evil against us? Be the head, by allowing God to chastise others. Yes, God helps those who help themselves, but he also empowers you when you bridle your tongue. We cannot say, do or even think things that will take us away from the love of God.

Knowledge and education are important in season, but overtime, it loses its value. Beauty gains great attention, but over time it all fades away. A 90 year old lady is not lying in bed focusing on her beauty queen days, her scholarships and awards or her genius intelligence quotient. Typically, what has value are the people who are still there, honoring her with their presence. On your death bed it does not matter, how many shoes are in the closet or how many diamonds are in the vault; what matters are the people you loved and the moments you shared. The healthcare that we receive in those final moments often reflects the care that we gave to others. Love is something we want to build, because it is the only thing that will sustain us, when we have nothing. February is the month of love, to learn more about the love of God and to show expressions of love and affection. The rest of the year is designed to put our love into continual and consistent action. Love is always in season; Love never fails.

Types of Love

Agape love if unselfish and represent true relentless love. This love expects nothing in return; it is a sacrificial love that reminds us of the love that Christ has for us. He loves us like parents love their children and overlooks our faults just as parents continually forgive their children's wrong doing. Agape love always holds others in high esteem. This love desires more for another person than for themselves – the greatest love. Satan does not want us to have Agape love, so he sends his fan club to weary you and to wear you down. Rest is very important to gain agape love. We become to weary because we strive with others too long. To keep your agape love strong, you have to set boundaries. You must know when to approach and when to refrain. Although you may be rested and have the agape, you can walk into territory where others have not completely refreshed nor rested in Jesus. We see the warning signs but think we have enough power in us to overcome evil with good old fashioned agape love. There have been times, when I walked into a room and felt the tension where the air was suffocating. I had to learn to make my appearance brief, cheerful and focused and depart with quickness. If the muck and mire get on you, it will choke the life out of you. To sustain agape, we have to yield to the warning. Make your love quick and strong, but retreat, when friendly fire is projected. We have to learn when to whisper, "I love you, just thought of something I have to do; God bless you, hope to see you tomorrow." Close the door gently and run to the escape route—don't let the issue take away your agape. Guard your heart, so Agape in you remains powerful and ready to love.

Eros love is a passionate love with sensual desires; a longing to be intimate or close. It represents a pure emotion without logic. Eros love can be platonic while recognizing God given beauty. Eros love is seeking to explore and find truth through transparency and openness. Spiritual truths are known and valued in the art of eros love. In eros love, we like people because they have the same backgrounds and goals and ambitions in life. Eros love cause us to sin and give away the valuable connections that God anointed and purposed for husband and wife. Eros cause us to dive into relationships that move us in the plan of Satan to kill, steal and destroy everything that was planned for our lives by God. Parents must instill a systematic plan early in life to program children regarding what to look for in a partner. Because there is often no plan or standard set, men and women fall prey to every allure that manifest in their presence. If the person that you commit to become intimate with, has a set plan only, to sample from a pool of applicants, then your plan to meet Mr. /Mrs. Right has already been swindled. You walked into an agreement that does not set you as a standard; you signed a contract with your lips, to be placed on the buffet line. The enemy often licks his/her lips to warn you that his/her appetite is ferocious and then, smooths his/her hair to let you know that he/she is more self-involved than focused on what's good mutually exclusive. Heed the warnings, check for the body language that says "It's all about me". Notice the little things that eros does, and ask God for wisdom to recognize a love that is not in his plan for you. After a one night stand, stop the pattern and don't fall for the same tricky approach. Satan uses the same plan he tried to destroy you with the first time. Given another opportunity, you may not survive. One third (33%) of my vinyl fence fell down/collapsed last year and I paid almost a thousand dollars to repair it or attempt to restore it. This year one fourth (25%) of the fence fail completely, but along the property line globally, 75% of the fence was damaged. I could put it back together, but it never looked quite right. It swayed with every wind that blew through. It was also more vulnerable and weak, that now it will kiss and go with any wind that comes through. Eros gets excited about everything. This is a good place to stop and laugh, by the way. We all have played the fool, with a bag of wind, talking smooth and blowing smoke. You can't find them in the morning, because they are gone home to their wives/husbands or other partners, friends and associates. When God sends a mate right for you ladies and gentlemen, he/she will want nothing in return. It's awesome to share, but true eros seeks everything for self and agape seeks nothing.

Philia love is a mental love of friendship and care. This love has a give and take component based on virtues, integrity, equality and loyalty. It is a general type of love based on fun and activities shared and commitment to family, community and friends. Casual lovers fall in the category of philia. People love each other and remain friends because they enjoy similar things and can trust each other. Philia love is good when we do not allow intimacy to creep in. I have had two male friend, who have been married for over 30 years. The relationships remain strong because there were no gaps for intimacy to set in. Had intimacy slid into the relationship, there would be thought of care and suspicion. Intimacy comes with expectation; but a true friendship is based on respect, admiration and fellowship. Sin causes us to look differently at friends, peers and associates. It causes people to investigate, wonder about their activities and to fret. During marital stressors a true friend can come to share their issues and seek wisdom or opinions from a true friend. This option is not typically available when friendships does not remain pure. Once I had a friend come for counsel, at the thought of a spouse's threat to separate. I could easily counsel and mentor this friend, because I had a mutual respect that was not contaminated by sexual intimacy. Moments like this threat of a major life change, teaches us the value of a loyal friend. If you only have ten people in your address book or mobile phone contacts and you have been intimate with them all, you have no line of emergency open for catastrophic events. It is time to clean out the contacts that hold you back and open up lines for wholesome friendship that you can reach, to share exciting news about your partner/ spouse and life events.

Storge love endures and hangs with the tides of life. This relationship of love is relevant to family and tolerance for the issues of family living. This love accepts people with their faults and continues to maintain contact out of community moirés. We are expected to keep loving children who disappoint us with deeds and actions. We are expected to tolerate siblings who leave us with the load of carrying for bed ridden parents. We must love them despite their unpleasant deeds. Some siblings test our patience and exhaust us with competitive spirits; however, we must love. Sometimes we have to love from a distance in order to stay in the will of God and the grace of God. If we are tested too frequently, sometimes we have to seek other opportunities to love, so we are not always striving. When we stay in the marrow of striving too long with people, we become stuck and stagnant. A dangerous place to abide. Endurance does not require that we remain in the eye of the storm; we can endure on the side lines, in the perimeters. We can be a telephone call away for special needs, but not make ourselves available for the sticky stuff. The spirit of God will let us know when trouble is coming, so pay attention and have an emergency survival plan in place. Let you love be strong and consistent.

The attached love survey will be used to rate each type of love based on the month theme to score your dominant love type.

Nippy Love Definitions

AGAPE: I spoke words of love with all my heart and unconditional love

EROS: I only loved them in their presence and never thought of them later

PHILIA: I loved them the same way they loved me

STORGE: I tried to love them by staying away from them or not talking smart to them.

Ten (10) represent the greatest love and zero (0) represent the lease effort given. **The Love Survey**: Rate each type of love based on the month to score your dominant love type. **SAMPLE ONLY**

Table 1: The Love Survey

NIPPY RATINGS 0-10 times 10= BEST 0=LEAST	AGAPE	EROS	PHILIA	STORGE	RATINGS TOTAL
JANUARY Unity	7	3	8	2	20/40 (50%)
FEBRUARY Love	5	8	9	3	25/40 (62%)
MARCH Purity	4	5	8	5	22/40 (55%)
APRIL Abundance	3	5	8	9	25/40 (62%)
MAY Completion	8	8	8	3	27/40 (67%)
JUNE Commitment	10	9	8	7	34/40 (95%)
JULY Purpose	10	10	7	5	32/40 (80%)
AUGUST Pruning	9	9	9	9	36/40 (90%)
SEPTEMBER Shekinah Glory	10	10	10	8	38/40 (95%)
OCTOBER Harvest	2	7	10	9	28/40 (70%)

NOVEMBER Gratefulness	9	9	10	7	35/40 (87%)
DECEMBER New Birth	10	10	10	10	40/40 (100%)
Annual Love Score	88/120 73% Agape	77/120 64% Eros	105/120 88% Philia	77/120 64% Storge	259/360 Total Love Rating 72%

The Perfect Love Story began with a sovereign God who created a world that was beautiful. All 10s would be beautiful as well as all 0s; however, the values in the chart are unpredictable and wavering. God created the world from a blank slate, so He is awesome in his ability to work with nothing. He also shows himself powerful with much; but a wavering spirit is difficult to help. Revelation 3:15-17 New International Version (NIV) [15] I know your deeds, that you are neither cold nor hot. I wish you were either one or the other! [16] So, because you are lukewarm—neither hot nor cold—I am about to spit you out of my mouth. [17] You say, 'I am rich; I have acquired wealth and do not need a thing.' But you do not realize that you are wretched, pitiful, poor, blind and naked.

Jesus said I wish that you were hot or cold. If you are lukewarm I will spew you out of my mouth. One of these loves should be all the way hot at its best, or all the way cold, at its least value. All tens would show that you are consistent in one category or the other and all 0s will show that there is no love at all, totally indifferent. God can work with indifference and he can work with all the way on fire, but it is difficult to work with people who waiver with every wind that blows through.

Practicing True Love

True love is the agape love of God. The God kind of love is filled with mercy and grace.

As we progress in age, love can be a beautiful sunset or having a friend to rock with, on the back porch. When I worked in Tennessee, I yearned to be in my Alabama home on my back porch in Tanner, AL. It was a place of peace and refuge for me. The row of trees in the distance, gave me fellowship with God and man. Breathing in the fresh country air gave me a solace. I longed for the brick wall on the deck that was visible from the family room window. Nature is the God kind of love that makes life easy and smooth. Agape love has no agenda and conjures up no false beliefs. The God kind of love thinks the best in any situation. When we finally get tired of the hard knocks and the bruises, we finally want to trust God for only the good. Don't bring me any bad news, I'm only ready for good, so I have to expect good. I have to learn to love unconditionally, even when it seems too hard, too tedious and exhausting. Yes, I have to love. True love gives and forgives. Let love flow so that it whispers back to you sweet nothings.

Living in Agape

To live in agape we must love even when we are cheated and mistreated. If there is no remorse, we don't have to lay down and take it, but we must have a heart to love through every phase of detachment and rebuilding. Maintaining joy, means you don't give it away no matter what happens.

This has been a tough year for me, but I still have the joy of the Lord as my strength. I'm happy and I know I must be doing something right, because Satan is very displeased with me. He has attacked me from every direction, but God has been faithful and set ambush against the enemy.

Resting in Jesus has to be a daily plan if we are to live in agape. Our bodies and our minds need rest to rejuvenate the spirit. To make our way straight, we have to be calm, lay down and count it all joy.

My son was going through job challenges and I began to pray and wonder about his state of mind. He procrastinated on responding to the allegations, which frustrated me some; but before I became too weary, he gave me simple messages to let me know that if he has nothing else, he has faith. God has never let Him down, so he is not interested in regurgitating the scenarios. Because of his faith, I decided to be patient and wait on God. In less than one week, he was called by someone who had watched his work ethics and wanted him on his team. This confirms, when two are on one accord, God will be in the midst of it all. Although the suffering was not long in this case, we have gone through times when the suffering was long and catastrophic. By the mercies of God, we endured and came out as better soldiers. We were blessed by better faith, better confidence and better hope. Because of longsuffering, we can love in some very peculiar and exotic places. We can put the game face on and smile and honor the most dishonorable. You are not the first person to make me suffer, you cannot take my love. I was suffering in the womb, suffering in the vault, afflicted and wounded long before I met you. I know how to allow patience to synchronize with endurance. I am redeemed, I am healed, delivered, saved and set free. I am no longer in bondage; you cannot intimidate me. I have liberty to stand, trusting and waiting on Jesus.

My kindness is how I press through the valleys and climb up the mountains. I put my traveling shoes on, so I can go the distance. You may think I'm cold and carefree, but I have purpose and will not let any obstacles divert my path. My path is straight in Jesus. Oh yes, I will be kind to you. I certainly know who is for me and who is against me, but my mind is made up to be kind, no matter what games people play. You are not playing me, you're playing yourself. I'm working the agape plan to build up my health, wealth, integrity and prosperity.

Don't mistake my meekness for weakness. Meekness is what I need for agape to rest on me. Meekness allows me to minimize the attack of the enemy and count it as nothing. Meekness allows me to override and veto your sarcasm and condescending tone. Meekness allows me to meet you where you are and jump over the foolishness and smile, thanking you for the journey. I could have kicked, screamed and hollered, but agape in me allowed meekness to surrender to the power of an almighty, all knowing God.

The first thing we should teach our children is to be gentle; Treat people with love and care. Gentleness allows us access to the heart and core of God's people. If we can be gentle when we are going through the channels of heavy hits, rock throwing, brow beating, beat down and separation, God has the power to raise us up to float ever so gently, above the atmosphere. Gentleness elevates us and propels us through the storm. Laying down and resting persuades God to allow the power of gentleness to bless us with wings to fly. Gentleness manifest the agape love that soars like an eagle, ever so swift and calm.

Faithfulness is the ability of God to bless us with abundant health during a disaster. When he does the impossible, he shows his faithfulness. Every breath hinges on the faithfulness of a sovereign God. I couldn't save my breath if life depended on it. God makes my breathing successful. Every move we make God is faithful. Sometimes when we have a close walk with God, he manifest himself through perceptual visions and visual projections. He sends messages in every venue possible. He can manifest in a glass of water to show you his plan, his displeasure and his purpose. If you are not a witness to this, you need to draw a little bit closer. He is faithful to do exceedingly more than we can ask or think. His faithfulness is incomparable. We learn to trust Him more because he already did more than we expected.

Too often we want to take things in our own hands, when God want to show off a little bit and let you know who He really is in power. Sometimes, we are so impatient that we want to solve every problem and every situation. We need more self-control and wisdom to let go and let God do it for us. Agape love means we love God enough to let his plan work independent of our participation. Stop participating and start celebrating much sooner. God knows you love Him, when you trust his plan and his ability to execute the plan for you.

Reaching for Love

Love is all around us and we should be prepared to embrace it. Moments of love are available and we look over them while focusing on trivial perceived defeats. Love whispers and beckons us to participate. My girlfriend called from Birmingham, AL tonight to introduce me to someone that she thought was a classmate. While working on various projects, this was a welcome interruption. The gentleman talked loud and spoke "I'm JL and I'm going to be your next ex-husband". He was so hilarious. Answering the telephone gave me this moment of humor that invites and sets the atmosphere for love to manifest. We exchanged college years and he said, "I was in the 8th grade when you started college", which is why I did not remember him. He humored me by saying, "Yeah I saw you on campus and you wouldn't speak to me, but now that you're old and shriveled up, you're trying to holler". My girlfriend said, "Oh no baby, you got the wrong girl." I echoed back playfully," Oh you are just right, for me to train". They rumbled with laughter over the phone lines. Taunting is a form of agape love, in the right context. He was a stranger that probably never saw me a day in his life, but was willing to share his joy through humor. Some would have been offended, but the love for my girlfriend is so strong that anyone she connects me with, will immediately get a fair shake. When you are loyal, your love is easy to identify because love is expected and whispered at the mere mention of a name.

God knows exactly what you need and brings it, in due season. He shows his love in the hearts and souls of our co-workers, associates, neighbors, strangers, family and friends.

Love speaks so many languages that it would be impossible to count; nevertheless love is available if we reach for it, whisper to it and embrace.

If we meet impatient and unkind people then we know we have a huge project forthcoming or we need to flee from the assignment. If it overloads you then there will be no love, peace or joy involved. Labor and resentment occurs when we try to force a bad fit. Putting a size 10 foot in a size 8 shoe is not going to happen. We try to make things happen that are never going to manifest. Read the label and you will know or you can waste precious time, trying to stuff inside the shoe. When a size 10 shoe fits a size 10 foot there is harmony and the atmosphere is set for love to manifest. How good the shoe look is irrelevant, if you cannot wear the shoe, it has no value. If you need a jogging partner then you will not be content with a person that prevents the run. It does not matter that they use to jet through and overshadow the competition, what matters now is what they can do today. We must train and prepare our hearts to love in excellence, so we are never defeated.

Summary and Conclusions

Agape love never fails. God love us and will not relent. His desire is that we love others as we desire to be loved. Press in and run the race with diligence and perseverance. We are charged to be the best that we can and hold a standard of love in all areas of life. We are all being evaluated and want the scales to show that our love measures up to the standard of God.

References: I Corinthians 13: 4—7 (NIV) Love is patient, Love is Kind …

Whisper: Word to the Wise

Vignettes III:
March Words of Whisper

Enrichment Topic - Cleansing Winds

Vignettes III: March Words of Whisper

Enrichment Topic - Cleansing Winds

Introduction: Cleansing Winds

If the son therefore shall make you free, ye shall be free indeed John 8:36 (KJV). Imagine being free, then imagine being free INDEED. The prayer of Jabez is "Oh Lord, bless me indeed". Jabez was praying for spiritual freedom, for liberty and the favor of God surrounding his life. His mother bore him in great pain, but he did not want that to be his life story. Often we try to endure too much, but Jabez decided the bulk stops right here. 1-Chronicles 4:9—10 (NIV) is the prayer of Jabez: ⁹ Jabez was more honorable than his brothers. His mother had named him Jabez,[c] saying, "I gave birth to him in pain." ¹⁰ Jabez cried out to the God of Israel, "Oh, that you would bless me and enlarge my territory! Let your hand be with me, and keep me from harm so that I will be free from pain." And God granted his request.

Imagine being blessed and then imagine being blessed INDEED. You are indeed God's son, Matthew 14:33 (WNT). Matthew 26:44 The spirit INDEED is willing, but the flesh is weak. Mark 9:13 (KJV)That Elias is indeed come, and they have done unto him whatsoever they listed, as it is written of him. Luke 10:2 (WEB) Then he said to them, "The harvest is INDEED plentiful, but the laborers are few. Pray therefore to the Lord of the harvest, that he may send out laborers into his harvest. We need an INDEED prayer sent to God. Indeed brings better than blessed results.

Who is the Holy Spirit?

Prior to Jesus leaving the earth, Jesus promised his disciples to send a comforter to dwell among his people. Many of us are not in tune with the spirit, because we don't recognize the realness and the availability. The

Holy Spirit is the person of God that enters inside our deoxyribonucleic acid (aka DNA). The life of man is consumed by the life of God and a merger of chemistry gives genetic information that links us to the heritage and kingdom of God. The more we read our bibles and learn of the nature of Christ, we can partake in the blood and cellular form of Christ as new creatures. The word of God cleanses us and washes off the sinful man and transforms us into sons of God. His body fluid on the inside of us, compels us to walk in a path that is pleasing to him. The blood of Jesus purges our iniquities makes us think, live, talk and walk like soldiers. When we go into battle, we want to fight like Christ. We need a parable on your brain or in your pocket. Your intelligence can set ambush against the enemy. The Holy Spirit will use any part of your body to speak for it. Your shoe can talk to you and give a word from God. Look at your eyes and see what God is saying. He already promise to use a rock to praise Him if you don't, so everything and anything is subject to the spirit of God. II Timothy 3: 16 (HCSB). All Scripture is breathed out by God and profitable for teaching, for reproof, for correction, and for training in righteousness.

John 14:1-31 (NIV) has application that is profitable. As you read, you should apply it to your daily living.

John 14
14:1 "Do not let your heart become troubled; believe in God, believe also in Me.

14:2 "In My Father's house exist many dwelling places; if they did not exist, I would have told you; for I go to prepare a place for you.

14:3 "If I go and prepare a place for you, I will come again and receive you to Myself, that where I have gone, there you may go also.

14:4 "And you know the way where I go."

14:5 Thomas said to Him, "Lord, we do not know where you go, how we know the way?"

14:6 Jesus said to him, "I proclaim myself the way, and the truth, and the life; no one comes to the Father but through me.

14:7 "If you had known Me, you would have known My Father also; from now on you know Him, and have seen Him."

14:8 Philip said to Him, "Lord, show us the Father, and we will consider it enough for us."

14:9 Jesus said to him, "Have I stayed so long with you, and yet you have not come to know Me, Philip? He who has seen Me has seen the Father; how can you say, 'Show us the Father'?

14:10 "Do you not believe that I dwell in the Father, and the Father dwells in me? The words that I say to you I do not speak on My own initiative, but the Father abiding in Me does His works.

When we do as God ask we are walking in the same power and authority as God. Reflecting in the natural on verse 1, If you believe in Ollie and Imogene (my parents, then you can believe in me. Verse2 My parents have made provisions for me to eat and sleep and to abide as long as I have need. Verse 3 My parents are paving the way for me that territory where they have trod I also have access. They also equip us to do more than they have done by pressing forward. Verse 4 My parents set the template, so I only need to duplicate to get results. Verse 5 Our parents showed us the way to go, if we would take heed. We have a role model somewhere to echo what to do when you don't know. A bible sitting on the table can show you the way. Verse 6 If you don't see anything in the natural to show you the way, look up, look at me says the Lord, I got you. Maybe your parents fell short and maybe grandma is gone, but I am always present, I am here, says God. Verse 7 If you had known Sandy and Edna Lucas (My grandparents), you would also know Imogene and Sharon, because I made them all. If Sharon walks in the room, she may sing the same songs Imogene sings, because she put it in her. Imogene may laugh just like Sandy because he put the same spirit of laughter in her. Influence is what Jesus is saying. He has influenced me to be who I am, so we are one and the same. When Benjamin rejoices, Sharon automatically rejoices, because we are one in the natural and one in the spirit. Verse 8 Showing Imogene is not necessary because I'm Imogene. She taught me, cloned me to have the values that she has. Imogene is Godly, so whatever she says, Sharon is going to say because Sharon is walking in the same path. Verse 9 How can you say, I sure would like to meet your mother? Jesus is saying, Why? He's just like me. Why? Imogene is just like me. She is going to say what I say, do what I do, because she put it in me. I look just like Imogene, stranger on the street, say, "Are you Imogene's daughter?" Oh yes the DNA is present and strong. And I plan to look as good as she does when I turn 75 too. Verse 10 Don't you know I cook my biscuits the same way Imogene cooks hers and clean house in the same pattern. Can't you tell I belong to her. Verse 11. She is at the church every time the doors open and I'm writing a ministry book---why do you need to see her? She is in me and I am in her. We look alike, we talk alike we smell the same because I buy the same soap and perfumes that she buys. Verse 12 Because I have observed Imogene I will perfect what she does and the spirit of oneness will press me to do greater things. Verse 13 I am Imogene Malone's daughter, I need access because of the blessing on her life. She was the community nurse, so I'm comfortable asking God for health, asking her old supervisor to give me a job. They know her so the apple does not fall far from the tree. She worked 40 years, so Sharon can be trusted to work at least 40 years and or multitask for 40 years. Verse 14 Mother I need shoes to go to school, work–to a banquet. I represent you—shoes granted. Verse 15 Because I love my parents, I comply with their authority. I follow instructions so the blessing of this household stays with me all my days. Verse 16 If my mother can't pick me up from school, she will send someone to get me. It may be a neighbor, friend, sister or co-worker, but she is going to send the help you need, when she cannot be there. Jesus said, I will send you a helper when I go away. Verse 17 If you trust the God that I serve, when all else fails, He will come to you and meet your needs. Trust God and not man. Yes it's great when man shows up but don't be weary when man fails, because God is better Verse 18 I'm putting God in you because when I'm not here, he can provide better than I. You will never be alone. That is the love of a parent—the love of God. Jesus gave us the father, who can perform more excellent than He in the natural. Verse 19 My father is gone to be with the Lord, but he sang and prayed early in the morning echoing all over the house, so now that he is gone, the spirit of God remains in me to give comfort and peace. Verse 20 Now that Ollie is gone, I can partake in the same assurance that he had. I can trust God to be faithful to my needs. I know that when I take Him into battle, I will have victory. Verse 21 On my father's dying bed, God showed me a vision of dad lying in bed carrying a heavy load, but Dad lifted his finger to heaven and said, "I know you still got the power". It may be my time to go through this season, but I know you are able to turn it around. I'm pleased with you, because I'm on your team. Whatever you do just keep me in your care. Verse 22 The world did not get my comfort – my advanced information was for me. God gave it to me because of my love for my father and my love for Him. Verse 23 God was faithful to me, he abided with me during a time of great need. Awesome savior, gentle redeemer manifested in me. He was there already, showing himself faithful. Verse 24 When we love Christ it's easy to say "No" to things that displease Him. When we love him enough to ask Him to remove our wicked desires, he is steadfast to do more than we can ask or think. Verse 25 Dad taught me the same message while he was living, but God put it in my remembrance on his death bed. Verse 26 God used my dad's message to remind me and comfort me that all is well. That's why people sing, shout and pray, "God is so faithful". Verse 28 Dad always said, "One day I'm going home to be with the Lord, but you just keep your hands in God's hand and everything will be alright. When I've done all I can do, God can do more. Verse 29 You already know in advance, so when it happens don't be alarmed. God comes in many ways, speaking all languages possible. He can use a bird, a tree or a bee-anything. It's already happened, so if He did it before, He can do it again. Verse 30 My sister's best friend died recently. She told her young daughter, "I'm going to bed now, and I won't get back up—Basically saying, I'm in another zone. So the message is to remember my teaching. Break the cord and detach. Now it's time to spread your wings. God is coming for me, I've done all I can do. Verse 31 I am walking in truth now. I'm doing what the Lord would have me to do. His will is done and I accept. This is the promise birth out in these scriptures revealing the heart and soul of God.

The Purpose for the Holy Spirit

The purpose for the Holy Spirit is to lead, guide and protect us from evil. The Holy Spirit reminds us of things we need to do, to be successful and put into memory what the word of God says and what we have been taught in daily living. In my dream, an iron gate that I purchased had been installed and was being shaken by the winds but it did not relent, it remained strong and did the job that I purposed for it to do. The fence was not delivered nor installed but God showed me that the plan was good and would work according to his power that he placed in the iron fence. This was comforting to know that God is giving me advanced information that whatever happens, this fence, this gate will stand. Prior to completing my doctoral degree, God showed me a score of 80% on my dissertation in a dream. This was enough to let me know I passed. You only get a pass or fail, so the score was symbolic of passing. I leaped out of bed at 3-4 am in the morning to check my email and the notice was right there at that moment, giving me the good news, that my dissertation was complete. The spirit is activated and He makes it abundantly clear that He is with me, fighting every battle. I never got the warnings before, so I asked Him to make my messages abundantly clear and so He is faithful to his promises and He certainly did and does that for me. He is no respecter of persons.

God will do it for you. I seek his face, I watch his hands and I look for my messages everywhere I go.

Receiving the Promise

In order to receive, we must stretch out our hands in an upward position. Reaching out and reaching up grants access to the wonderworking power of God. If you need him, you need to reach with boldness and confidence. You have to believe that you belong to him. I am fully persuaded that if I need anything that Imogene has, it automatically mine. Imogene has imparted God in me, so I also enjoy the pleasures of the Kingdom of God, a secret society of a land flowing with milk and honey, unspeakable joy and treasures forevermore.

It's so simple, but we make it hard. Big mama said, "If you make your bed hard, you got to lay in it." We lay in hard beds when God has a feather floating air mattress in the balance. Reach to heaven and gain access to all your desires. God is faithful and no respecter of persons. You will be treated just and fair-the promise is yours to receive. God says, "I will not leave you nor forsake you." I am fully persuaded that he means every word He says. I receive the promise, by expecting it. I meditate on my hearts' desire, I take action and let his plan unfold. I don't force anything to go my way. I like to see the end from the beginning, but when the end is not visible in my bank account, I follow the unction of the spirit. Everything that I desire manifest in a dream, vision and the imagination of my mind, so I trust God to receive. I drove 20 miles sometimes 3 times a week for a year to sit in the drive way and look at the house I wanted. Today, I'm living in that house because of my heart's desire. I purchased a magazine and looked at Hawaii until purpose manifested that quickened me to purchase a plane ticket and reserve a room. Several people spoke about going with me, but they all cancelled. It was not in their heart, but the magazine put it in mine. Preparation for the promise is key to receiving the promises of God. Your mind has to be ready to handle the consequences that come with the assignment. I had to be ready to go by myself. My plans were not predicated on what someone else did or did not do, I trusted God. The same principle applies to everything we need in life.

How to manifest the power of the Holy Spirit

After God breathed a fresh cleansing wind on Jabez, the curse of pain disbanded. The Holy Spirit can do miraculous things if we have the humility to ask. We need some audacity to get the authority of God working for us. We need to summons the spirit of God to show up and manifest a wonder working power. Your petition and prayers in sincerity with boldness and passion gets God attention.

How to live in the Spirit

Living in the spirit is living in power. Living without the yoke of fear, lack and condemnation. God I love and adore you, please show me how to enjoy your promises and not be afraid. Some are so accustomed to the yoke that they don't know how to live without sickness, disease, poverty, discrimination. I rebuke all evil from my life. I rest in you to fight my battles. I am an overcomer by the blood of Jesus and by the words of my testimony. The greater one lives on the inside of me. I am blessed to be a blessing. I trust God. My affirmation of what I desire will take me to the power of God. I live a holy, sanctified and joyful life because I walk in faith. I don't worry about my mistakes, I keep pressing towards the mark.

When the blessings come, I am faithful to hear the voice of God quickening me to do his will with the resources I have. I watch for his miracles, I watch for His presence stirring the fountain of my circumstances. When the yokes fall off, I fall to my knees and praise

God, worshipping Him for being truth and freedom. I live in the spirit by bridling my tongue. Everyone cannot receive what God is doing.

How to purge our sins with the help of the Spirit

We cannot make ourselves free. Only Christ can activate a healing power in us. Only the Holy Spirit can give us a quickening to do something before we have time to think about it. Once the spirit comes alive, there is nothing you can do to relent. The Holy Spirit is so excited to get out of the box that things start happening like magic. Blessing come from every direction. Studying the bible, practicing the presence of God, living a holy lifestyle and seeking God's approval with every decision we make, will guarantee activation of his power. With every blessing, Satan sends a test, so buff up and prepare to win. Greater test may seem catastrophic, so much that you wonder what you did wrong. Usually you did nothing. Satan needed greater ammunition, because his pebbles just bounced off, because of the word in you, the power and authority in you. So now he's shooting bombs, so we need some bomb power. We must keep taking our faith higher to offset his attacks. Gird up your loins, with God all things are possible. The blood of Jesus makes your power more dynamic INDEED. Partake in the blood of the lamb to purify your hearts and minds. The blood on top of love, on top of faith, on top of desire gives the INDEED revelation of a mighty in battle God.

Walking in Restoration

Walking in freedom comes with a cost. Condemnation comes when the spirit of God breathes a fresh wind on you. You may have to do things that are unusual as the cost for your anointing. That's when we have to profess, "Greater is He in me, than He that is in the world". Separation comes with the anointing, so it's important to like being with yourself and God. We have to go through the wash, rinse and spin cycle to be a vessel fit for Kingdom usage. Even then, we may get folded or hung in the closet waiting to be picked. Some stay in the closet for years and never get used. Others are folded and hid in a drawer. Sometimes, they have to be traded out to another owner, another church to be used by God. Nevertheless, being prepared for the assignment is what God is seeking.

The word sustains us through victory and defeat. Some become humble when they are called, some haughty and others are out of position. Some must wait for their purpose to manifest. When God assigns a task, he will equip you to complete the task without help from anyone. He wants the glory. When we try to push the task on others, we fail. My wholeness depends on my boldness to go alone. If you cannot go alone, the vision will not tarry. I keep trying to get a team together to manifest my invention idea. God keeps diverting the process, because everyone cannot comprehend. I spoke to a few people about marketing my book, but soon realized, God wants the glory. He wrote it and he is not sharing the glory with anyone at this time. I'm going to wait. It took 20 years to get serious enough to pull the book together, so I will wait for his perfect plan to market it. It's all about Him, so why would he not take it and use it to build up His kingdom. His power indeed is greater than any channel I can turn to move forward. I walk in his plan and purpose and abandon my thoughts to do anything. It's not about me, so I'm trusting God to go the distance. I rest in Jesus, I listen for his voice and I follow his instructions. Restoration remains steadfast, when we stay in the breath of God.

Summary and Conclusions

Some people have lived the easy life and took no risk so they have no battle wounds to mention. Praise God they learned a straight path early on with wisdom, knowledge and understanding making intercessions for them all the way through. Many of us did not go the straight easy route. We had GPS (parents, grandparents, family) but got mixed signals that took us to Australia, when we were trying to get to Birmingham, AL. Strong Pentecostal like ministry is necessary for the world, who is wounded from head to toe. We have no time for a cute sermons and flipped up hair dos distracting our focus in church, when we are wounded. If you never been wounded you can't tell anyone how to be healed. Take advice from the wounded to heal your wounds. The wounded can tell you how the fresh wind comes and how to prepare for it.. Healing comes with pain and itching, soreness and oozing of sticky matter. It comes with discomfort and groans. We must stay encouraged because it is just a process. The healing wings of God can make your eyes itch, your nose run, your teeth ache. Your shoulders cramp and your feet may swell—but it's just part of the process. Clean the body, clean the mind with the word of God and the blood of Jesus, the spirit then obeys and the soul becomes free.

Reference: II Timothy 3: 16 HCSB). All Scripture is inspired by God and is profitable for teaching, for reproof, for correction, and for training in righteousness.

Vignettes IV:
April Words of Wisdom

Enrichment Topic: The Outpouring/Showers

Vignettes IV

Enrichment Topic - The Outpouring/Showers

Introduction: Walking in the Rain

The month of April is a season to receive showers of blessings from a sovereign God. As laborers for Christ, we should prepare to be consumed by the mercies and favors of God as he seek to bless his people. It does not matter what work you do, all of the work on earth is purposed for the kingdom of God. If you ask for blessings at this season, God is distributing; all we need to do is lift our hands to heaven and ask, "Lord, give me and my family, my children, my nieces and nephews, cousins, friends rain in the time of the latter rain; Please Lord make flashing clouds; Give us rain, grass in the field for everyone. The Lord will affirm your petition by making flashing clouds; He will give us showers of rain, grass in the field for everyone", simply by asking. In April, during the showers of rain, just ask God to bless you in deed. The rain is evidence that He has showers to give.

The Lord prepared you for this season of his clouds of outpouring of righteousness. What better time to pray than when the showers of rain are pouring down. If you have put seed in the ground, it's the best time to seek a harvest. Often we pray during the storm, to help us survive the storm, but God wants us to thrive in the storm. We need to fall to our knees and ask for great and mighty things in the presence of the storm. The earth is opening up and your salvation is bearing fruit, even in the midst of calamity, God created you for light breaking through, in the darkest places. God does the most tragic things for his beloved, so that we may know that (Isaiah 45: 6-8) from the rising to the setting of the sun, there is no one besides Him. He is the Lord and there is no other. He causes well-being and creates calamity; the Lord who does all these things. Praise God for His mysteries; when people think you are down and out, God raises up a new standard.

Preparing for Leadership: Spiritual Blessings and Spiritual Things

In Isaiah 45, God is calling King Cyrus to know Him; He anoints him to be a deliverer. Cyrus was a Persian king, a pagan who had unmerited favor with God. God used Cyrus as an instrument chosen to do His work. In this case, God chose a foreigner and anointed him with oil to do His work. Cyrus was walking in bad territory, but was walking in the reign of God, so God used His power to cleanse Cyrus in the midst of the enemy. Appointing Cyrus was unacceptable to some people, who deemed themselves more worthy. Some people today think they should be in your position, standing in your designated pulpit, enjoying your wife or your husband and living in your neighborhood, in your house, going to your job and taking your vacations; but God appointed you. The least of the least, you were given the assignment. The LORD did not set his affection on you and choose you because you were more numerous than other peoples, for you were the fewest of all peoples (Deuteronomy 7:7, NIV).

When God appointed Cyrus as King over the persian people, little did he know that along with the assignment, he would also become King over the jewish captives. When God puts us in authority, it is often a set up for additional responsibility that we do not anticipate. Often we are the unlikely candidate, but God said, "I choose you", and there is nothing anyone can do about it. You may not be the cleanest knife in the drawer, but you are the chosen one of God. Cyrus was a dignitary of strategic military deployment and was established as an advocate for human rights-bridging eastern and western cultures. Proverbs 21:1 (ASV) states that the King's heart is in the hand of the Lord; He directs it like a watercourse wherever he pleases. Accepting the call to be Kings and Queens, makes us all fit to carry out the assignment of God.

God sends notice to prepare the way for his blessings. It may come in a dream, through a word of knowledge, but surely God makes his plan, his divine word known unto his prophets (Isaiah 44:25—26). God called Cyrus by name so there would be no mistake that His authority was imminent. Cyrus publicly credits God for his edict to free the Jewish captives from Babylon. God commissioned Cyrus to destroy the bars of the Babylonian prisons, so His people would be made free. He trusted his humility as a King to follow orders.

To become a leader, we must first know how to be led, how to hear the voice of authority and thus knowing how to hear the voice of God. One hundred fifty years before Cyrus was born, Isaiah predicted that Cyrus would free the Jews. After 70 years of bondage, the Jews were allowed to return to freedom to Israel, under the authority of King Cyrus. Although Cyrus was not in Christ, Christ took authority and showed his sovereign power that Cyrus would willfully do as God pleases. Sometimes we do the right thing when the wrong thing is in us ... that's when God executes His sovereign power. Don't take credit for it, because only God could quicken you to act on His behalf. That's his executive clemency to bring order back into your lives. He pardons us without our petition. He pardoned Cyrus, so Cyrus could in like manner pardon others.

Typically when a person wants a clean record (exoneration), it's necessary to obtain character references to send a petition to the Federal Bureau of Investigations to perform a background check to set you free from all convictions and past sins. A United States pardons attorney has to review notarized affidavits validating you as worthy of forgiveness and then submit documents to the governing body, the President of the United States of America. This did not happen for King Cyrus because God usurped the authority of man and gave Cyrus clemency by his executive power.

President Barack Obama was given clemency by God's executive order. Whatever people tried to find wrong from his past, God wiped his record clean and placed him in authority. We need to pray for executive clemency to usurp Satan's control in our lives—submit your application for pardon to God. People who are not anointed with wisdom can only hurt you and put you in more bondage; they are hurt and want to share the pain. When God gets involved, he breaks every chain. He used King Cyrus to break the bars open. God removed the chains off Cyrus and King Cyrus proceeded to use his new found power to remove burdens and destroy yokes off the Israelites. When you are empowered with freedom, your freedom will work for anybody in proximity of the blessing. They can have the same privileges, honor and blessings that you have. A full unconditional pardon and restoration of all rights can be yours. Because you are connected to the right King, you can also have the resolve, restoration of your good name and occupational rights and potential that you desire. That is the mercy of God. Prepare for his outpouring showers of blessings and dominion.

Preparing for Wealth and Health

Whom the son sets free is free indeed John 8:36 (KJV). When men and women are released from prison, drug addiction, sex addiction, gambling addictions, etc., previous partners are often ridiculed for seeking to know them. If we read the word of God, we would know that when God sets a person free they are free in deed. The best man you can find is one who has been released by the power of God. Not everyone is released by God, but everyone released has anointing to be restored. Who we connect with upon release determines the benefit and level of restoration that we can enjoy. If you reject your friend, your husband or your wife at this time of release, you forfeit the health and the wealth that was promised to you as matron and patrons of God.

Your blessings can be transferred to another willing vessel appointed by God to carry out the assignment. Wisdom tells you where you are supposed to be to receive your blessings. At the right brook, God promises to sustain us. Waters will not flow if you are standing at the wrong well. We must hear the gentle whisper of God mandating us to be where he prefers and not where we think is right. God's ways are not our ways, his thoughts are not our thoughts. We must ask for wisdom and wait to get the unction of God to move and make every decision in our lives. Your health and wealth depends on your willingness to hear and obey God.

The Roles of the Umbrella in the Natural and in the Spirit

The purpose for the umbrella is to take the pressure of the rain off your head and allow it to fall in the direction of your feet. As long as the water is at your feet, you cannot drown and there is no threat of danger to your life. Just like the excessive rain, God puts the enemy under your feet. Your feet can absorb it or you can tilt or move the umbrella in the direction that you choose to offset the water.

God takes the weight of the outpouring of his blessings off your head, so that you will not be overcome with flooding and torrential weathering. Too much of a good thing can weigh you down, even when it's from God. The wisdom of God is symbolic of an umbrella that opens up just when you need it and it sustains you by directing you where to carry it and the direction to hold it for maximum benefit. Without wisdom to use the umbrella properly we can still perish with the blessing in hand.

When God towers over us, he will protect us from burdens that try to press us down. He keeps us fresh and dry, so we do not appear to be whipped wet. Even good things can be too much sometimes. We love our families, but sometimes we need God hovering over us to set ambush against the showers of family issues that manifest. We love family, but sometimes we need a covering over us to protect us from the overflow of family crises and emergencies. God can give us the glory without the shame. He hovers over us because we are vessels fit for his purpose.

We must petition God's presence to lead the way through every season of life, so we will get victory down every avenue that we travel. Don't drop the umbrella when the rain is sure to come again. We need God on the good days to strengthen and prepare us for the bad days. If he stays with us, we don't have far to call for his immediate intervention. Leaving your umbrella in the car is no use to you when you are in the work building. Everyone else need their covering at the same time, so you can't borrow my God, when I need him for myself. You must take ownership and have the faith that I have to get the benefit of the covering of God that I enjoy. We must be ready in season and out of season. Take God with you everywhere you go, then he will be ready when you call.

Chasing after the Dream

Pay attention to your patterns in life. The last success achieved will likely determine how the next success is coming. We can aimlessly chase the dream or we can rhythmically and systematically capture the essence of the dream that we preference. We are just a prayer away from the prize. A whisper to the Father can end the chase. Walking into your season includes a time of prayer and sacrificial offering unto God. The right seed will manifest the fruit which satisfies our hunger and longing. Just being in position can give you the same empowerment that King Cyrus had in setting the captives free. Your mission in life is directly connected to your victory.

I listed my house with a realtor for two years and had no success, during the years of 2002–2004. I pondered the issues and every time, I thought of listing it again, God said "NO". I finally decided to flow with God to see the purpose for his persistence in telling me to keep the property. After the house flooded from a collapsed hot water heater (2009), I upgraded the floors and was satisfied to remain there and enjoy life. I added hardwood floors, removed wallpaper and painted all the rooms, put back splash ceramic in the bathrooms and kitchen and replaced all the dated lighting. I sat down one day with a sigh of relief and thought, "This is good" (May, 2011). Exactly two weeks later (May 27, 2011), a tornado came and demolished the home and every house on the street. Then I transitioned into an apartment for one year. My heart and my car, kept going back to a house I saw in a neighborhood that I could not dare imagine for myself. Finally, God removed the weight from my mind and moved me into a new home. Although it seemed that my labor was in vain, God showed me the work he was doing, where I could have sat patiently waiting on Him. It doesn't make sense to work, while God is working—nothing you do is going to last; that was the time to rest. Nevertheless, He restored me more than I could ask or think, inspite of myself.

I had to study long in College with challenges to get the harvest at one time; another season I had to just wait, lay on the floor and let the storm pass while trusting God; and yet another season, I had to fast and pray–communing with God for the manifestation of my harvest. One season took one hour to pass, another season took six years, another took six days and yet another took twenty years. God is faithful, no matter how long it takes. Through every season, he met all of my needs. I never lacked, his provision was present and right on time. I have to remind myself and others, that if we have not changed, then neither has God changed his love for us. If we don't move, God's blessing will know exactly where to find us. The blessing usually comes at the same place of your obedience to Christ. Once you truly know God, your only requirement is to be where God desires and let the dream find you— right where God wants you to be.

Spreading Favor and Distributing Grace

Once the merciful dew of the Lord's presence rains down in our lives, we are held to a new standard of living. 1 Peter 5:10 (KJV) reads, "But the God of all grace, who hath called us unto his eternal glory by Christ Jesus, after ye have suffered a little while, make you perfect, stablish, strengthen, and settle you." If we get what we deserve, we will never come out of bondage and captivity, but because of God's grace, his mercy is new every morning, we can enjoy the quiet release of his whisper, when we offer up our prayer to Him. He gives us grace—His unmerited favor. He spares us the punishment that we deserve with His mercy. Because he is just and filled with favor, we must show ourselves faithful to show favor and grace to our fellowman.

We are called to honor each other, to esteem one another and to forgive. We must not hold back favor and grace. Even when person's that we give favor to, do not favor us, we must be steadfast. Even when the ones we love, love someone else, we must hold on to our convictions. My friend (in Tuscaloosa, Alabama) always says, "I'm rolling with you, right or wrong, I love you and you have my vote, my approval". She says "I may not agree with you, but I'm rolling with you". Her love transcends all the issues. My joy is hers to honor; likewise, her joy is mine to honor. If you fall, we will be together is what she says.

As Christians, we need to love each other better, stop criticizing each other and have true unconditional love. You can't distribute grace and talk negatively about things that other people do and say; You can't distribute grace when you sneer at the mention of someone's name; grace can't manifest in you as you work against a plan that someone designed to help us all; and surely you can't distribute grace when you do not study the word of God to show yourself approved. We have to practice being soldiers for Christ. We have to endure and suffer for righteousness sake; then we will be established and blessed by God; He who sustain us.

What to do when the rain keeps pouring down

Sing, dance and shout, because the Lord is good, faithful, kind and worthy of all praises in heaven and earth. After you have suffered long, you know how to rest in the rain; the flood does not overwhelm you, because you have been established in patience. Once patience has it's perfect work in us, we become ENTIRE-COMPLETE, wanting NOTHING (James 1:4 NIV) Let perseverance finish its work so that you may be mature and complete, not lacking anything. When we allow patience to have its perfect work in us, then there is now no thing that we cannot acquire. We are now equipped and balanced to contain the overflow of God's grace and mercy. Because we have been faithful over a few things, God has now made us ruler over much. Matthew 25:23 new living translation (NLT) states, "The master said, 'Well done, my good and faithful servant. You have been faithful in handling this small amount, so now I will give you many more responsibilities. Let's celebrate together! When the blessings of God come we need the wisdom of God to lead us in the truth of God's purpose for the health and wealth. How we use the mind and body of Christ determines how long we will enjoy and partake in the blessings of a sound body and mind.

Summary and Conclusion

I've noticed that when people esteem others, they keep going from blessings to higher blessings; from victories to higher victories–The rain just keeps falling down over their lives. The motor is so strong that prominence is on automatic pilot; those people couldn't stop it now if they wanted the blessing to stop. Once a clock is wound it's going to keep moving until God says it's enough. A full tank of gas can last a lifetime with God in the engine. When you mess with God's people, you are standing on holy ground. When you mess with God's people, you are messing with God; we are holy, you can't mess us up. In like manner, any Christian that you come against will automatically deter you from the promises of God. God does not relent on his grace and mercy. God's honor to us is equivalent to our praise and worship to God. We must put in enough worship to last for many lifetimes. We must take notes and honor others to sustain the life for ourselves and for many generations to come. It's not just for you, it's for the nations. Be showered with blessings in Jesus name. Scriptural References: Zechariah 10:1 (KJV) Ask ye the Lord rain in the time of the latter rain; so the Lord shall make bright clouds; and give them showers of rain, to everyone grass in the field.

Whisper: Word to the Wise

Vignettes V:
May Words of Wisdom
Enrichment Topic: Preparation/Graduation

Vignettes V

Enrichment Topic - Preparation/Graduation

Introduction: I'm Ready for the Challenge

The month of May is Mental Health Awareness month. It is action packed with worldwide graduation ceremonies and Memorial Day homage. A season where we celebrate many stressful outcomes, that makes us humble, grateful, happy, sad, fearful and glad. All the mixed emotions, set the atmosphere for great uncertainty whereby, the sky is the limit of what could happen next. Graduation is a time of fear, anxiety and exhilaration. At the point where you want to give up the most, signals the ending of an era and the beginning of new territory to explore and conquer. May is typically a month of readiness, where persons have to stand firm in the promise and pursue the final outcome measures of their assignments. High School students and College students all over the world are often frustrated during the early month of May, because this is the time of reckoning. The darkest times typically come, just before daylight. The mathematical calculations are sometime unclear and so close to the point of deliverance that one wrong move will change the fate of what is anticipated. It is an unnerving time at best, because life changes are exhausting and stressful, even when we expect greatness and honorable skills of preparation. We must be ready for the challenges that comes before the victory.

How to Plan for the Future

I Corinthians 15:58 (KJV) "Be ye steadfast unmovable, always abiding in the works of the Lord, for as much as ye know, your labor is not in vain, in the Lord." Planning for the future involves taking a daily perspective and reminder of the landmark that we are hoping for. We need a visual of what the other side will look like, feel like and taste like, so we can began to savor the moments of crossing over. A visual makes everything fair and worth the effort. In the crevices of your mind, you need to know that one plus one equals two. We want to know that studying today and forsaking parties and games will yield a final fruit of completion. This celebration of completion opens up a world of opportunities that could not be realized without first experiencing the dream and having the vision.

Knowing my Assignment

Body, soul and spirit must be in sync every day to yield the fruit of the assignment purposed by God. Some lived in divine purpose because it was natural, it was smooth and flowed easily from the essence of their being. They did what they were purposed to do, traveled the paths that God purposed exclusively for them and left no stone unturned. They often do not know the call, but they lived what felt right because the innocence of God lived and breathed within them. I attribute this to proper training in each season of life. Divine order was present in the womb, in the delivery room and in the home and community life. Parents, family, neighbors and community imparted the love of God during every stage of life, yielding the perfect will of God in good measure. Persons who flowed in this zone did not deviate from the throne of grace. Their network and prayer circle of support was best fitted to keep their minds in harmony, thereby birthing hope and optimism.

Ruth lived an honorable life before God. Ruth exceeded expectations and allowed the plan of God to manifest. Ruth remained committed and endured to win the prize of distinction. She was a beautiful and honored bride of Christ. When we honor God, He will honor us and exceed our expectations manifesting more than we can think or imagine. Ruth was not trying to bring attention to herself. She tried to be invisible doing her job quietly-gleaning in the fields. In obscurity, she was recognized.

Some of us are so blatant, we never get noticed. Isaiah 26:3 King James Version (KJV)

³ Thou wilt keep him in perfect peace, whose mind is stayed on thee: because he trusteth in thee (NIV). We acknowledge that perfect peace, perfect love and perfect harmony belongs to all who keep their eyes on the prize—Jesus Christ and his perfect plan. Decisions made from the core of our souls with the grand design of the spirit of God gives us the victory.

No one can beat you at being the best that God planned for you. Many finish the call of life without ever knowing their assignment—often because they stepped into the plan of another person, another sibling or associate. Collaborating with the mood of the crowd often leads us away from our purpose. In those moments, people are so confused and lack cohesion with body, soul and spirit. Days occur where living in the zone of flesh creates hazard, recklessness and self- destruction. Life is fuzzy and we feel our way in darkness, making mega mistakes along the way. Proverbs 14:12 states, There is a way that appears to be right, but in the end it leads to death (NIV). If we are living a dead life, we must reassess whose life are we living? Whose shoes did we step into? Then we can repent and move forward.

Pursuing the Mark

Philippians 3:14King James Version ¹⁴ I press toward the mark for the prize of the high calling of God in Christ Jesus (KJV).

Mental Health and physical health is necessary to receive from God the coat of righteousness. On the road between Jerusalem and Bethlehem lay the grave of Rachel, wife of Jacob and mother to Joseph and Benjamin. Jacob now has a total of twelve sons and is grieving the loss of his wife. At age seventeen, Joseph had to travel past his mother's grave to become the man that God designed for him to be. The road to success often leads to opposition, challenges and sometimes bereavement. Fulfilling the purpose of God does not exempt us from trouble, but we must continue the journey past the trouble to reach the perfect design of God. Because Joseph was the first born of Rachel, he was the favorite of Jacobs' twelve sons and the youngest son, Benjamin, who was born just before Rachel's death was highly favored by his brother Joseph.

The older brothers were jealous of Joseph because he was favored and given a special coat of many colors by their father. Joseph had dreams and special gifts and knew that he was in line for the favor and special appointment by God. The brothers became weary of his favor and insights and decided to abort the plan of God by leaving Joseph in a pit to die. Joseph was ready for greatness, but did not perceive the detour that he would have to endure before moving forward to the plan and purpose of God.

We are ready for completion but are sometimes too close to the edge to pass the final test of endurance. Some stayed in the safety zone and feel confident that at their worst or at their best performance, they still have an assurance that they will survive, reach the mark, graduate and transcend to the goals of their aspirations. This signals a time of confidence, anxiety and fear. Confidence is for those who have planned well and have no doubt that the end result will be celebrated. Others have anxiety that perhaps they walked too close to the edge, missed too many assignments along the way and are worried that they cannot recuperate the errors of their ways. The third group are in fear that there is no grace, no mercy and no possibility of measuring up to complete the process and requirement for commencement.

Jacob could have felt defeated, but he kept his eyes on the perfect promises and will of God. At his father's request, Jacob traveled fifty miles alone to check on his ten brothers in Shekem who were tending flock. They were in Dothan, which caused him to travel 15 more miles to check on his brother. When he became in view, one brother states, "Here comes the dreamer". Imagine that, because God is speaking to you and prophesying his plan, your siblings are now jealous, your co-workers are now jealous, your neighbors don't want anything to do with you. They say, "I don't fool with her because she is driving a Jaguar, A BMW or a Bentley. She said that she is going to get a church and be Pastor— what a dreamer." Joseph's love gave him strength mentally and physically to endure. Your love will sustain you when the nay-sayers come, when the isolation comes, your love will keep you in perfect comfort.

As long as you have a car, you have friends, but when they get a car you can't get a ride and can't sit on the leather. That's the pit, that Joseph endured not losing sight of God, the love and plan of God.

Joseph Dream #1

Joseph said, "We were binding sheaves of grain out in the field when suddenly my sheaf rose and stood upright, while your sheaves gathered around mine and bowed down to it." Genesis 37: 7 (NIV)

Joseph Dream #2

"I had another dream, and this time the sun and moon and eleven stars were bowing down to me." Genesis 37: 9 (NIV)

When you share your dreams, you risk jealousy and fear and you risk detours to the plan of God. People don't want you to have power and authority over them, particularly when they are older than you and think they are smarter than you. Even his father rebuked the idea that he would have to bow down to his son and that his son Joseph would have authority over him, Rachel and his brothers.

Reuben has planned to double back and rescue his brother Joseph from the pit, but while he was gone, his brother decided to sell Joseph to the Ishmaelite's. No one wants to be sold, but if we know the plan of God, we should wait patiently for the promise to come.

Persevering when the Task is Too Hard

If we could turn back time, perhaps we would have sought a mentor, set a calendar of priorities and burned the midnight oil more often, so the fear does not consume and overwhelm us. We always knew that we wanted the prize, but in our imaginations, we believe that having immediate gratification, fun and exhilaration was more pressing and urgent than preparing for the elated final Friday in the month of May. Although the task was hard, Joseph had to endure; you also have to endure. We have to stand on the promises of God.

Completion: Graduation Celebration Commemoration

Of course we want everyone who started with us to finish with us, but at this final moment, everyone has to give an account for him/herself. At this critical stage, there is no time to pull up another, because we are all consumed with pressing in for the prize; presenting ourselves as holy, acceptable as our reasonable service.

Group one and two typically are affirmed; although some only by the grace of God and by miracles, signs and wonders. The third group are typically denied the blessing of crossing over to the next phase of life. The good news is that if they don't get weary in doing well, they will reap also, if they don't give up. One more semester, one more year, may be all it takes to receive the final blessing at this season in life. Some needed 100% on the last exam, project or test, and pressed in to win it. They finally put their whole heart in, because they decided not to be left out of the esteemed commencement ceremony. Memorial Day has come and we celebrate the season of completion. We prepare regalia, invitation and commence to a new level in life, as we walk past the grave of suffering and pain.

Walking in Victory

Joseph was a good soldier, a highly skilled veteran, a drum major for righteousness, forgiveness and deliverance. Despite the opposition, he became ruler. He was in the pit, he was destined to die, there was a cover up where his robe was torn and dipped in blood to validate a story that he was killed by wild goats. Despite the weapons of warfare, Joseph stayed on course. He received the promises of ruler ship as he dreamed.

Summary and Conclusion

We all want God to say "Well done!" The graduation tassel represents the crossing over–completion. To graduate from one season to another season we must allow the hardships that come to perfect us to completion. When God gives us his plan, we don't have to share it with everyone, we must allow the plan to happen without distractions. We can delay the plan, others may try to abort the plan, but if God leads, he will perfect every plan that he designs and orchestrate it to completion.

Reference: I Corinthians 15:58 (KJV) States, "Be ye steadfast unmovable, always abiding in the works of the Lord, for as much as ye know, your labor is not in vain, in the Lord."

Whisper: Word to the Wise

Vignettes VI:
June Words of Wisdom

Enrichment Topic: The Bridal Commitment

Vignettes VI: June Words of Wisdom

Enrichment Topic - The Month of Commitment

Introduction: The Proposal

The month of June signifies the first month of the summer season and is equated as a popular month to get married. I will always remember my childhood pastor Elmore Hurt telling the story of meeting his wife and marrying her on the fourth day. Jesus got up on the third appointed day, but Pastor Hurt needed one more day. He was certainly flowing in the Holy Ghost. They were on the fast track for commitment. When we speak of love at first site, tremendous information is processed in the mind. People often say, when I first saw her, I knew that she would be my wife or when I first saw him, I knew that he would be my husband. The spirit, mind, body and soul made an immediate connection-in this case a lifetime connection. Pastor Hurt and Mother Martha were instantly committed to each other and synchronized to go on a journey together never looking back-but moving forward. They were seasoned and ripe for picking. They had the mind of Christ in oneness and remained together until death parted them, far more than 50 years together.

When you pick a seed, you must follow a process of planting, fertilizing, watering, preparation, husbandry/cultivation and excavation to make the vineyard estate prominent and ready for presentation. However, Pastor Hurt chose a luscious fruit that was already processed and completed the cycle of orientation. Mother Martha, chose a pear ripe for pulling off the vine. When there is love at first site then the proposal is already established in the heart. Many times we dig up a potato and have to let it slowly evolve, but if we wait too long the potato disintegrates, collapse, crumble and breaks down in numerous ways. Pastor Hurt did not allow any air to flow between himself and Mother Martha, therefore, no contamination could get in to create atrophy. He had the maturity to know what he wanted and she had the preparation to receive the blessing of uniting with him—and it was good. As women we have to learn to whisper and reason with our men, contenders and husbands, so that we do not show ourselves openly rebellious. Had Vashti explained to her husband that seeing her unclothed would cause other men to lust after her, perhaps King Ahasuerus would have relented. Either way a lesson is learned that we are all dispensable at a moment's notice. Life is not always going to be fair, but our confidence must be in God and not in man. At the very request, Vashti's beautiful body broke out in hives, perhaps to validate her feelings that the request was sinful and wrong.

Esther (the replacement bride of King Ahasuerus) was of Jewish heritage, although she lived in ancient Persia, was left an orphan and raised by her cousin, Mordecai. Esther was made Queen from the pick of 400 virgin ladies with great beauty. Many of the ladies had passed up previous opportunities and now find themselves in a line up whereas, if not chosen, this will be their last chance to be married. Esther was given favor because of her faithfulness and the season of her exposure. Sometimes, local girls push away the blessing, so foreign girls show up to gain favor with the King. Often we lose favor because we are loud and condescending; God is telling us to whisper with wisdom and kindness. Surely his favor and power will manifest, as we develop a gentle whispering nature. In today's society, Caucasian females have increased favor with African American men. These Men have decided that they prefer the white female because she acquiesces to their authority. African American females seem to be more embarrassing and condescending towards their authority, so men seem to defer to diverse ethnicity females as their preference. God is pleased when we comply with authority; He is likewise pleased when we do not yield to a sinful nature. A line has to be drawn in the sand, when the behavior and the request borders on falling out of favor with God. Listening to the spirit of God, allows us to put the brakes on in adverse circumstances. In the long run, it's best to quietly wait and trust a sovereign God to redeem us. Some invitations we have to politely whisper and decline. Women of all ethnicities are allowing men not only to expose them publicly, take photos of their private body parts and sending them across the worldwide websites, but they are also allowing them to video record intimate sexual acts that should be private and honored in a marital relationship. We can't call it exploitation, because they are 30 years and older, profiling and talking into the cameras–willing to be mocked. There is no shame, no remorse and they actually think that they are being honored. Now, what have we taught them at home? Why do they perceive pornography to be humorous and exciting? Where did the church go wrong? How did this creep in? Maybe, while we were focused on money or perhaps ridiculing the youth ideas and contributions– while we failed to train them for church ministry and leadership. They found a place to shine in the gutters of the world, because we rejected them in the church. We must esteem the youth, encourage them, love them, teach, train, build them up and prepare them for success in life. An invitation must be given early, so the season does not pass.

The Engagement Party

In preparation for the royal party to acquiesce a new bride for the King, all of the ladies washed and cleansed to beautify themselves to present themselves as the best pick. As a contender for the King; Ladies presented their best graceful styles, profiles, hairstyles, best royal attire and adornments. No one was concerned that they could be as easily replaced as Queen Vashti, they merely wanted the title of being the Queen and living a Queen's life, even it was only for a season. If she was replaced with all of her glory and beauty, why do we think that we too will not be heart broken and dismissed. Regardless of this, the party continues with all of its glitz and glamour. We think that a fortune 500 Executive Leader, an Engineer, Doctor, Lawyer, a wealthy man, an NFL/NBA player, A military Officer, A College Chancellor, Senators and Congressmen, President of the USA, King of Persia is the best thing going and yet, so many honorable men sit on the sideline observing thousands of women parade for one perceived stately man.

Many of those wives and companions are the most miserable women in the world. Nevertheless, the celebration for Queen continues, to find the most worthy of all the female candidates for King Ahasuerus. The party was most impressive of all gala events, the King was astute at entertaining and showing off the grandeur of his palace–his kingdom. Yet, the party continues with all of its excellence and finally, Esther is chosen among the 400 female competitors. The remaining 399 women were basically hidden and never allowed to marry anyone. Esther was appointed to serve as Queen, at the King's pleasure.

In today's society women do so much to gain favor. We lavish with body scrubs, shower gels, bath bombs, fragrances, elegant hairstyles, fashions and jewelry, we frequent the nail shops and the weave bars, we get college degrees and try to gain equal approval and it's still not enough. Only the party we prepare with God as the honored guest will get us the desires of our hearts. We still celebrate because we are overcomers.

Knowing How to Walk Together

About ten years ago, a handsome gentleman at least 20 years older than my mother approached me at church and said, "How are you young lady? You know I would love to have your mother if she would take me. I have enough to take care of two people nicely", he said. I smiled and thanked him for appreciating my mother's beauty. Those words forever resonate in my mind. At roughly 85 years old, this handsome older man still has an eye for beautiful ladies and the desire and respect to take care of one special lady. Exactly his idea of what enough is to take care of two people, I will never know, but the concept that he understood his role as a man was heartwarming for me. This man still had enough money to live and share with someone else, likely because the desire was in his heart. He passed away shortly after that and I never saw him again. Nevertheless, what he did for me that day, took my breath away. He made a lasting impression that as a woman, I should be valued enough that someone would desire to share the fruit of his labor. Love makes a man desire the best for a woman. Love makes a man honor a woman and desire to be his companion in life. Not that women are not designed to share, but the thought that a man is so chivalrous and brave to take on the needs of a beautiful woman. God has to honor and respect the very desire of his heart. I feel certain that on earth and In heaven, God gave and will give this older gentleman more than he imagined possible.

Over generations, this mindset of picking a fruit ripe for presentation has changed and become tainted in so many forms and fashions, with ludicrous and illicit tactics foregoing any humility and sincerity to honor the essence of mere eye contact. Pastor Hurt looked into her eyes, her beauty and disposition and he saw the essence of what God had prepared for him and he wanted nothing more than intimacy and cohabitation with her. She glanced at his stately manner, his approach, handsomeness, his gentleness and looked no further, because she could only imagine him as the best fruit on the vine. When you know you have the best that God prepared for you, then there is no requirement or urgency to pick and taste another apple, another apple and yet another apple. After tasting so many apples, none will have any special quality, they will all seem common and it will be difficult to pick the best one.

Accepting the Invitation

An invitation is a call to manifest the desires of the heart. Invitations beckons and beseech one to come hither to connect to the plan and future that is available for such a time as this.

Esther 4:14 notes, "For if you remain silent at this time, relief and deliverance for the Jews will arise from another place, but you and your father's family will perish. And who knows that you have come to your royal position for such a time as this?" The story of Esther is letting us know that when invitations are sent we must be prompt and on point to flow in the path of God's promises. You can overthink and undermine who you are in Christ and miss the most dynamic season of a lifetime. The King of Persia, Xerxes threw a gala event and summoned his beautiful bride to show her off to the crowd. Queen Vashti refused to humor her husband's request and was overconfident of her power by one measure, but expressed wisdom to not put herself in a sinful position. Because she publicly embarrassed the King, he disposed of her and called for a royal pageant to select his new bride. Although Queen Vashti accepted the prior invitation, her attitude caused her to lose favor with the King and her invite to be Queen became null and void. Her title made her feel overly confident to speak her mind publicly.

Walking in Sync with God

Walking in Sync with God will give a measure of success that last through eternity. Commitment to the plan and purpose of God allows us to present ourselves as a living sacrifice to God, holy and acceptable, as our reasonable service. When we commit, we lay down our will and allow God's will to take over. We must be strong in the Lord and in the power of his might. When we are determine to succeed, we usually do, because the God in us empowers us for success. Imagine when God wills something to happen, the mere thought can cause a volcanic explosion and the idea will manifest. We must ponder the will of God to set in motion the power of God working in those things that we seek to accomplish.

Commitment

Commitment means that we are in for the long haul. We are not discouraged by discrimination and aggravations, systemic rearrangements and competition. If God is for us, He is more than the world against us. God will sustain us, when we feel like the least of the least. His strength is made perfect in our weakness. I have to commit to his authority. I need his might working because it takes a little portion of His might, whereas, my might takes a lot of calculations, reckoning and configuring. Often my might still does not add up, but a bit of God's might is always excellent and forthcoming.

A man is appointed as leader and Lordship over the home. Choosing a fearless leader to rule over your household requires the mind of Christ. When we choose what we think is good, it often goes corrupt. The Groom's role in the marriage is to make decisions that are in everyone's best interest. King Ahasuerus decision was designed to serve him-his pleasure. That was his legacy and that was all he could perceive. Generational legacies can create destructive patterns to persist for many generations. Once the pattern is established, only the might of God can reverse it, because patterns and habits are hard to break unless God gets in the motion of the cycle. The brides' responsibility is to submit to Godly authority. When his authority takes precedence over the authority of God, then women are covered by the mercy of God to reject wrongful authority.

Ruth 1:16-17 (NASB) But Ruth said, "Do not urge me to leave you or to return from following you. For where you go I will go, and where you lodge I will lodge. Your people shall be my people, and your God my God. Ruth exceeds expectations and follows her mother in law after the demise of her husband. In chapter 2 of the book of Ruth, Ruth is building relationship and dedication to Boaz. God is pleased with her attitude and character. Ruth supersedes the law mandates and humbles herself by asking for what she is already entitled to have. This mighty move captured God's attention and qualified Ruth for explosive-phenomenal favor with God. Ruth 2:8-9 Then Boaz said to Ruth, "Listen carefully, my daughter. Do not go to glean in another field; furthermore, do not go on from this one, but stay here with my maids. "Let your eyes be on the field which they reap, and go after them. Indeed, I have commanded the servants not to touch you. When you are thirsty, go to the water jars and drink from the servants draw." Ruth 2:10 Then she fell on her face, bowing to the ground and said to him, "Why have I found favor in your sight that you should take notice of me, since I am a foreigner?" Ruth 2:11-13 And Boaz answered and said to her, "All that you have done for your mother-in-law after the death of your husband has been fully reported to me, and how you left your father and your mother and the land of your birth, and came to a people that you did not previously know. "May the Lord reward your work, and your wages be full from the Lord, the God of Israel, under whose wings you have come to seek refuge." Then she said, "I have found favor in your sight, my lord, for you have comforted me and indeed have spoken kindly to your maidservant, though I am not like one of your maidservants.

Ruth 2:14 And at mealtime Boaz said to her, "Come here, that you may eat of the bread and dip your piece of bread in the vinegar." So she sat beside the reapers; and he served her roasted grain, and she ate and was satisfied and had some left. Ruth 2:15-16 When she rose to glean, Boaz commanded his servants, saying, "Let Her glean even among the sheaves, and do not insult her." And also you shall Purposely pull out for her some grain from the bundles and leave it that she may glean, and do not rebuke her." Ruth 2:17-19 So she gleaned in the field until evening. Then she beat out what she had gleaned, and it was about an ephah of barley. And she took it up and went into the city, and her mother-in-law saw how much she had gleaned. She also took it out and gave Naomi what she had left. Her mother-in-law then said to her, "Where did you glean today and where did you work? May he who took notice of you be blessed." So she told her mother-in-law with whom she had worked and said, "The name of the man with whom I worked today is Boaz." Because of the grace of God Ruth was given exceedingly more than she could ask or think. She was in awe of the favor of Boaz. She wondered, what did she do to gain such favor. She simply humbled herself and asked very politely, and did not remind him of what she was entitled. Therefore, she got much more. She was redeemed. The Right to redeem is given to the closest relative. Is God your closest relative? The kinsman redeemer must be able and have the resources to redeem us. Can they pay the price to redeem us? Did God pay the price? Is the kinsman willing to redeem? They must have the heart and love to redeem. Yes, God has the love to redeem us. Boaz immediately recognized Ruth's character and wanted to know who she belonged to. The kinsman redeemer was ready to stake his claim on her. When she approached him with humility, he opened up his heart to give her the best provision in the field, water for her thirst and protection from harm. Ruth and Orpah both had a choice to make. Orpah went back to the familiar. Ruth chose to follow the path of honor with Naomi –that led to favor and honor with God and man (Boaz), where she laid on his threshing floor and gathered the harvest.

Summary and Conclusions

Your Threshing Floor may be a tornado, hurricane, earthquake, forrest fire … Your threshing floor may be depression, cancer, addiction, bereavement … Other sickness, disease and infirmity. Your threshing floor may be lack of housing, money, resources or joblessness. Your threshing floor may be lack of a friend, companion and relationships; nevertheless, refinement will come when you rest in Jesus. How you rest on the threshing floor determines how you reap during the harvest season. The harvest season always comes. Count it all joy because the testing of your faith worketh patience and when patience has its perfect work, you will be complete, entire and wanting nothing. According to Maya Angelou, renowned poet, "Love liberates". Boaz love for Ruth liberated her and gave her a new life in Christ. Commitment empowers us to prosper in all venues. A gentle spirit whispers an invitation for greatness.

Reference: Ruth 1:16—17 (NASB) But Ruth said, "Do not urge me to leave you or to return from following you. For where you go I will go, and where you lodge I will lodge. Your people shall be my people, and your God my God.

Whisper: Word to the Wise

Vignettes VII:
July Words of Wisdom

Enrichment Topic: Mission Accomplished

Vignettes VII: July Words of Wisdom

Enrichment Topic - Mission Accomplished

The best work year of my life was serving as the Director of Counseling and Career Services for Martin Methodist College in Pulaski, TN. During this one year season, I perceived that I was empowered to excel as an independent professional. God released me from judgement, the rod of correction and gave me wings to soar to any level that I could achieve. I was validated as a professional and was given free rein to develop a counseling and career services center, while I taught psychology courses at this esteemed and honorable college. I gained a notable cultural experience and received an impartation from God that gave me strength to weather many storms that came on my journey hereafter. The year was amazing and fruitful; I met people who made lifetime impressions on my self-worth and value as a professional. A dose of God that most people never claim to enjoy, in a town that had a perceived tainted history. I now understand that I was on the fast track and God wanted me to glimpse his mercy and grace, to feel his presence and know that he rises above every circumstance and situation. On this college campus, God expressed clearly, "I am God, I brought you here so you can experience my love on a different and unexpected platform". There was no condemnation, only expectation that I could and would do the job that I was hired to do. Reflecting on the acceptance makes me humble. I was given the great and very important task of planning the freshman orientation, preparing computerized vocational testing for all graduating seniors, job placement and exit interviews. These were all task that I never did in the workforce, but had the vision and the enthusiasm to know that I could do it, enjoy it and be a blessing to the student body in the process.

Walking in Purpose

My purpose for that brief and exciting year was to experience new heights in God and to show love to people who may not have experienced love and support without a personal agenda. I walked in my call, fulfilled my assignment in one year and was transitioned to new and greater assignments. A one year assignment can be amazing, but even more so amazing when one has the fortitude to complete it and trust God to move forward in His plan. My family were a blessing to me during this season, Pastor Benny Waddle Sr. and Mother Deloris Waddle. I was honored and embraced as a daughter and will forever know the love that was given freely.

I wore many hats during this season and was grateful to change the hat of Instructor, Freshman Orientation Facilitator, Exit Counselor, Testing and Placement Professional, Personal Counselor, Career Counselor, Academic Advisor, Mentor and Life Coach.

As an instructor I taught chapters in psychology to students from many origins and ethnic backgrounds and presented so that no offense could be perceived or conceived. As freshman orientation facilitator it was an honor to plan activities to introduce new students to college life, career options and cultural events to promote a balanced and intriguing environment for work, adventure, fun and play. I really enjoyed being an exit counselor, because it was very exciting to know that seasons were ending with so many possibilities for future career and life success. Exit counseling is also enjoyable for the students because they are very proud of their accomplishments and know that if they completed this difficult task, then they are capable of so much more. College life exposed many more good things happening, than bad. Although students, faculty as all people were faced with challenges great and small. Exit counseling can be sad because many of the students, you will never see again. This is why a follow up program is so important. My role as Testing and Placement Professional pushed me into a zone of loading software onto about 30 computers in a computer lab to determine the best attributes and career fit that best match each student. Planning to examine over 100 freshmen required coordinating and maneuvering in a new way that my career duties had not previously braved. I wondered how did they know that I could do that? This is a huge job to trust anyone to achieve single handed. But the challenge was completed and each new carrot that dangled in front of me I savored. Being an academic advisor means you get to share your wisdom, your experience and instincts paired with a standardized test that gives options for future career success. It's extraordinary when your words of whisper, reaches eager ears and humble hearts. The maturity of college students offers more honor to their Mentors because they are there by choice and not by government mandates. They often empowered themselves to come and desire to get the best opportunities while they are enrolled. Too often teachers and caregivers are oblivious to the challenges that students face and misinterpret failure as lack of motivation and laziness. Serving as a master's level clinical psychologist prepared me for insights on student emotions. It also inspires students to feel that you are safe to talk to about those emotional issues, as well as the academic challenges. Students are not privy to just simple relationship problems, but many are faced with serious domestic issues, psychiatric disorders and financial stressors. They are still in the real world and have to deal with sickness, disease and death being imminent and actual. Life is throwing curve balls that some assume will stand still until they finish college. College is difficult on a "normal day", but paired with schizophrenia, a personality disorder, compulsive behavior habits that peep into the scene, it can be exasperating. Some students endure public humiliation from random psychotic outburst that cause them to publicly rage on the campus grounds, and yet the following day they have to present themselves in class as capable and strong. Older adults adapt quickly and move on because, they have learned that life goes on despite what we have to deal with. Older adults know that God's promises to not put more on us than we can bare. Older adults know that God will give us beauty for ashes, strength for all fears, gladness for mourning and peace for despair. However, most 19 year old students are still terrified to the point of anxiety attacks that someone will recognize them as that person, who had a fit of rage, who vomited in the parking lot, who had seizure activity in the classroom or couldn't stop laughing or hiccupping for a year.

Partnering with the Student Support Services department gave more empowerment for student success. Students enjoyed the best of academic support and were valued as key players in their future achievements. Galatians 6:9 compels us to not grow weary in doing good, because in due season, in God's perfect timing, we will reap a harvest of blessing, if we remain committed and don't give up. It is a phenomenal blessing to see the end, of a season of success.

Staying Focused

We are charged to do our parts and let God do His. As young professionals, we typically expect to have simple duties and become overwhelmed if we are asked to perform additional task; however, as we become more mature and more confident we are ready to pass the test to achieve everything that God need us to do. We don't fully understand that we are working for God and not for Man. Whatever we do, God ask us to do it as unto Him. When we do our work, as unto the Lord, then our challenge does not linger. I worked as unto the Lord and soon after qualified to move on to new territory in which to plow and plant more seed. II Timothy 4:7 states, "I have fought the good fight, I have finished the race I have kept the faith". Working in this environment planted the seed for my future academic success.

Victory in Jesus Christ

The best lesson that can be whispered in your ears is "Don't stop". You have to encourage yourself, no matter what, "I will keep pressing forward". The race is not given to the swift or to the strong, but to those who endure until the end (Ecclesiastes 9:11). This simply means keep getting up, keep planning, keep studying and God will intevene on your behalf. Of course you cannot do what seems impossible, but God can. Stay in the game and be on His winning team.

Summary and Conclusions

Many college students have graduated because they remained on course, they kept the faith and trusted that they would finish, if they never quit. Too often we think we have to do it, but you are just a vessel for God to achieve his purpose through. It's not about you, it's about kingdom living. It's about allowing God to do it. Don't fret, it's God job, not yours; it's God's final exam, not yours. When you allow God to finish the assignment, all you can do is salute Him in honor of his mighty work on your behalf. When the assignment is complete you can move forward to new territory. He will keep you in perpetual success, when you follow His plan and allow Him to order your steps.

Reference: II Timothy 4:7 (NKJV). I have fought the good fight, I have finished the race I have kept the faith.

Mission Impossible Ministry Skit

This skit was developed during my four years serving in prison ministry with a church group. This skit may be used as a teaching tool for all Christian audiences and aspiring believer groups.

A creative play director can take this prototype and make it as unique and personal to move forward the message of Christ that you desire to produce and share with others.

Mission Impossible Ministry Skit

Conference Call (Phone rings) Agents gather in board room (2 Agents)

Voice Speaks to Agents: Good Morning Mr. Househam/ Your mission should you accept it, is to recover a stolen item designated M Kiara/ Kumara (A heart symbol-principles of loving kindness, compassion and mindfulness). Evacuate the confine of (Metropolitan Correctional Center) MCC Chicago of a male inmate with proof that he is not guilty. Minister salvation in preparation for the court hearing, Secure gainful employment for this gentleman, restore the family division and have this unit at Sunday Service promptly at 9:30 a.m.

You may select any two team members. The third should be Mi Zelda Williams-Falls. She is a civilian, a highly professional thief and a smooth facilitator.

Mr. Burgess, the next time you decide to go on holiday, please be good enough to let us know where you are going. You have 48 hours to recruit M Kiara. As always if you disclose your assignment, I will disavow all knowledge of your actions. This message will self-destruct in 5 seconds.

Mr. Burgess: I will let you know where I'm going, I won't be on holiday.

Mr. Househam: We've heard of M Kiara. It's going to take more than a defibrillator to bring him back. We accept Sir.

Video comes on 5-4-3-2-1 POOF!!! (message self-destructs) Shows on BIG SCREEN at church with special effects

Mission Impossible theme song plays briefly with mission impossible video clips.

(Mr. Househam calls Mi Selda Williams Falls and recruits her expertise to join the team)

Mr. Househam: Ms. Falls I am calling to enlist your expert knowledge of property retrieval and solicit your support with a mission to evacuate a gentleman from the local detention facility with the white glove protocol and enforcement of the code of restoration.

Mr. Burgess: Paces the floor alone and mutters "How did he know I was on holiday". Shakes his head.

Etc. etc.

Team Attire (EVERYONE): Black pant suit, white shirts, red necktie (males and females), black shoes, black socks and dark sunglasses/shades, white gloves.

Sergeant comes out with instructions to chief Agent

Chief Agent: Good Afternoon Sir.

Chaplain Attire: White pants/white shirt with a captain's hat

Chaplain: We expect you to follow the rules at this facility

Chief Agent: Yes Sir

Chaplain: Start on time and end on time, we have a schedule to maintain

Chief Agent: Yes Sir

Chaplain: Prays for the team ministry success

Etc., etc., etc.

Roll Call by Chief Agent: Theme music plays softly

Each member comes out and turns back to audience in a vertical line.

One by one they step forward pivots, turns to face audience with feet together and one additional step forward with a stomp.

Each Agent: Name is called says "Present and Ready"(After final stomp facing audience)

Chief Secret Agent # 1 talks to the TEAM about Spiritual Warfare and gives assignment

Mission impossible music plays as team comes in and plays again as team rushes out to fulfill the mission.

Chief Secret Agent # 2: Okay good people, we are here on assignment to remove burdens and to destroy yokes etc. etc. ... Talks about Spiritual Freedom

Team: Yes Sir

Team Chief Secret Agent #1: We came to break the revolving door demon, castrate the criminal rate and annihilate the poverty

Minister the word:

In the 25th Chapter of the book of St. Matthew, Christ taught of the final judgment. When the Son of man returns in His glory according to the bible those who will enjoy eternity with him, will be those who followed his teachings.

In verses 36 - 48 Christ specifically states that those who minister to the captives, to those in prison will have a place with him in His Kingdom. "And the King shall answer and say unto them, Verily I say unto you, In as much as ye have done it unto one of the least of these my brethren, ye have done it unto me." Matthew 25:40

When you minister to those in prison, you minister to Christ and fulfill His law of love.

(Read also Luke 4:18 – 19 and Hebrews 13:3

Minister on the condition of the heart

Chaplain: Does the white glove test to check if inmate is innocent or guilty -- ready to go to court. Checks for all fruits of the spirit.

Inmate goes to court wearing his spiritual resume: Carrying a mirror signs all over him/her with photo in picture frames. (Decorated in fruits of the spirit)

Song: I'm looking at the man in the mirror by Michael Jackson

Patron at Freedom Booth: Inmate goes to both for patron to set him free

Patron at Job Booth: Inmate goes here to get a job and re-established into the community.

Family Booth: Inmate rejoins family: Inmate and wife excitement and pray together

Song: Play "Never could have made it" –very briefly

TEAM: Go back in to rescue another inmate

Song: Mission impossible music plays every time TEAM enters or exits

End with an upbeat freedom song (I made it)

Couple: Shows appreciation to the team for rescuing the family

SONG: Song by inmate spouse "No way I'm living without you"

Play CD and let someone else act it out …

Record a DVD of mission impossible scene (save it on the lap top to show on the big screen to accentuate the skit, during the announcement.

Suggested Song: Not Guilty by John P. Kee

Someone comes to administer the white glove test to a new inmate.

Inmate: Failed the white glove test.

Voice speaks to Agents: Your operation was poorly conceived and manifested. I expect perfection … bring in Agent Mi Selda Williams Falls NOW!!!

Two people back at board table.

Mi Selda Love injection: Shoot em up with the word. Hidden in a bible cage.

M Selda appears

Captain: Where is your badge mam?

Mi Sleda: "I should be on the list". I have the beloved KiMara/Kumara (Broken Heart) a Dove would be a good. Dove represent spiritual freedom. Play flying doves on Big Screen.

Announcement: Announce that we are accepting applications for secret agent team members for the spiritual freedom ministry etc.

It is important to emphasize, every Christian is called to service, but only you can decide what area of ministry God has called you to and whether or not you are willing to wholeheartedly make the commitment to operate in your calling.

We encourage you to simply count the cost before you make a commitment to join and serve in ministry. Start by reviewing the requirements set forth in your church covenant.

God Bless you always. Be encouraged, Whom the son sets free is free indeed.

Voice: II Timothy 4:7. I have fought the good fight, I have finished the race I have kept the faith. Word to the Wise ... Mission accomplished.

Vignettes VIII:
August Words of Wisdom

Enrichment Topic:
New Beginnings/ Planting Season

Vignettes VIII: August Words of Wisdom

Enrichment Topic: New Beginnings/ Planting Season

Introduction

Have you ever noticed that some students get to class early to speak with the teacher to sow seeds of commitment? Some do it with finesse and others don't find it necessary. Absolutely it is the season to plant seed, it is a new beginning, but it's important to research the soil before you plant seed. You can't plant into all soil and sometimes the seed receiver (soil) is already programmed to reject the sower because their seed has a reputation. My son learned from experience that it is best to inquire about his college instructor's background and ratings information before he signed up for the class. This allowed him to make better choices for instructor's who would captivate his ability to learn and thrive in the course objectives.

Likewise, in Sunday school, some students approach the teacher early to project what they want to happen and the focus that they want the teacher to take the class. They are not looking for a grade, but seeking influence over the classroom instructor. They don't want to teach, but want input for how the class operates. A wise teacher takes authority, yet empower all students to play viable roles. It's difficult to teach with opposition, but it can be done with the word of God (sword of the spirit/the gospel of truth), the helmet of salvation and the breastplate of righteousness. Unless a seed is planted in fertile soil, it will not prosper. This is a new season to plant and we should be subtle enough to receive and wise enough to plant in fertile soil. Whisper your seeds to the wise and not your weeds. Most qualified teachers know the difference. The month of August represent new beginnings and we should be wise and prepared to sow good seeds.

Setting Goals

A well designed plan will always work, when the worker follows it and cultivate the soil. When we purpose to work for the Kingdom of God, he will lead, guide and direct us into all truth. If God has paved the way for us, He will preserve us, when we remain steadfast in His plan. If He puts an impossible dream in us, then we have no right to fear or dread when the plan does not appear to be working as we prefer. The sovereign plan of God has no boundaries. When setting goals for God, He sometimes leads us into situations that become so sticky, that we cannot pull away from them easily. We may taste the honey although we know it's time to walk away from the hive, because the assignment is complete and it's time to tread new endeavors. Nonetheless, we are lured back in by the whisper of our church families, co-workers and friends. People chant things like, "You will never find another job this good that pays this much; you best stay where you are and leave good enough alone; If I were you, I would keep my tenure and stay where I am". But God is nudging you to trust Him and move in His more perfect plan. We hear God whispering, but the noise of the crowd takes over the gentle unction of God.

Sometimes we consider the medical needs of family and friends, we consider the location of college for our children and we back down because we want to remain in convenient territory. We sometimes hear God, but we focus on the boundaries, in the retirement plan in front of us. I'm very guilty of that mindset. I have twenty-seven years employment and could have retired at twenty-five but thirty look so much better on paper. So we linger on in a path that may not be the will of God. Holding on to bad soil, although the harvest seems profitable. We set our goals for selfish reason and do not comprehend the power of God. When he leads your decision, nothing you have in hand will compare to the good things that He is preparing.

Planning for a Future Harvest

Now that you understand that God does not want you to be stuck, lifting your feet up and not moving, walking in truth but bouncing back to mediocre surroundings; teaching your best and not prospering; preaching with power but no burdens removed and no yokes destroyed; counseling but no reconciliation; engineering the best plans, but no skyscrapers appear—now it's time to plan for fruit to abound. I know that you are walking under the assignment of God, but too often we think there is only part I and maybe part II. After we follow His path the second time, we think we have to remain status quo. When the spirit gets restless, it drives us to plow new territory, to set new goals. Jeremiah 29: 11 reads, "For I know the thoughts that I think towards you, saith the Lord, thoughts for peace, and not for evil, to give you an expected end". God cannot fail because He is the master planner. We are guaranteed winners when we allow Him to lead in his way and in his timing. Nothing is too hard with God.

Cracking the Soil: Getting to Know you

Now you are standing at the top of the mountain and no one is with you— it's time to let the memory of friends, family and loved ones go, in order to reach higher for the galaxy that has been prepared for you. On the mountain top, you can still pray and surrender your will to God. We can crack the soil of indecision on our knees. God answers prayers quickly and teaches us many things when we humble ourselves on our knees. I know you have accomplished a lot and more than anyone else in your circle, but is it enough for God. God may not reveal the answer, but he will guide you to the next step. Your obedience puts pressure on the end goal to manifest. It will erupt like a volcano spreading fertilizer over the land. This nourishment heals every situation and overflows so much that you cannot contain it. The shell of the situation is hard but inside the will of God, you will find rest, peace and pleasures forevermore.

Go ahead and trust God's plan, walk in truth, crack the shell open and experience the wings of God, where you will soar like an eagle.

Breaking the Yoke: The Courtship

In this land of prosperity, the yoke is easy and light the way God said it would be, but it's a little gooey and we don't' quite know what to do with it. Prosperity is overwhelming and we fear the unknown. We are in a new season of life and the news of your new directions are spreading and decisions have to be made. We've never had this much seed before, so we are getting calls, emails, text messages and voices from every avenue possible. During this season we are compelled to hear God over the messages of the world. Satan is making his bid to devour, so you come back to poverty and give victory to his plan. God is calling us to come higher and we have to be sensitive to his gentle courtship. We have to commune with God more and let his instructions unveil as only a bridegroom can appreciate. Enter into His rest and trust His plan. Everyone knows that when you are dating, you cuddle and look for the best that your friend has to offer. Now it's time to lay in the arms of God's rest and trust Him with your heart. The more we trust Him, the more He shares the secret things with us and allows us to enter a deeper season of bonding with Him.

Bonding: Soil and Seed

Now it's time to be balanced and methodical. With God, there is no urgency, simply a roadmap. His plan is revealed in patience and in steps, praise and worship. We step to his instructions. We use his people to activate the plan, we honor Him for His presence and as we journey, we never consider the obstacles, but praise Him for each victory. The seed of God's word must resonate in our hearts everywhere we go. We cannot afford to be distracted by what seems like words of condemnation, but take the good out of every conversation. We have to learn to separate the essential from the non-essential. Pluck out the not so good things and savor the blessing. A heart of gratitude will comfort you and give you rest. Be thankful in all things. Christians are to be offended by nothing, but sift out the best that can be found, dispel the hard grain in preparation for the harvest.

Commitment: Knowing how to irrigate and navigate

We are treading new territory and so the heat is going to turn up, just as it did for Shaddrach, Mechach and Abdenego in the fiery furnace, we are going to need the angel of God to show up and orchestrate some magic. When you have prayed before the heat turns up, God will lifts up a new standard on your behalf. It's amazing that all you need to do is stand still and be cool. All you have to do now is stand in attention, like a soldier. Your praise rains down the grace and mercy of God's presence. You should start practicing now, so you don't revert to the world's sassy look, but the confident look of knowing your heavenly father. Practice looking unmoved, unafraid, indifferent, loving and kind—even when the heat is three times hotter than it ought to be. Navigate with meekness and don't change your posture—just be cool.

Merger: Packing /blending the soil

Darkness cannot comprehend light, because light represent the omnipresent, omniscient and omnipotent power of God. Rain water cannot be comprehended by a blazing fire, because it will consume and defuse it on all test and trials. God says test me and see that I'm good. You are no match for God because he absorbs your venom and makes it sweet. A merger with the power of God will always be unified with the whisper, wisdom and plan of God. Your soul will find rest, when you trust in God.

Soil, Water and Sunlight Empowerment

Soil has the ability to reproduce anything planted in like kind. Powered with water it has more potential to grow and reach higher levels. A little water can grow a little mixed with the soil of meekness; another measure of growth comes with the soil of gentleness, a different measure of growth comes with the soil of thanksgiving and respectively with all fruits of the spirit: love, peace, longsuffering, goodness, faith and temperance. The added component of sunshine's affect, give vitality and life to all dead things planted in the grown. The sun penetrates and motivates the product to reach greater heights with less effort. The son of God does that for us as well. Once the spirit of God plants the seed in our hearts and we embrace the idea or the plan of God, He works the plan in us and uses us to manifest his outcomes that benefits our lives. Pruning the offspring gives liberty to drop more seed to bring forth new birth.

Summary and Conclusions

Wisdom teaches us that the battle is God's, not ours. We worry but God already has the solution. We rush from bank to bank, door to door seeking people to solve our problems when God already has the plan in hand. If we learn to rest and consult with our father, He will guide us into His will. When things are not going as we planned, we should stop to consider God's plan. When resistance comes overtime, we should seek God again for guidance to the next phase in life. Be encouraged that new seasons in God's plan, brings a reward of great recompense. In Jesus.

Reference: Jeremiah 29: 11. Jeremiah 29: 11 reads, "For I know the thoughts that I think towards you, saith the Lord, thoughts for peace, and not for evil, to give you an expected end".

Whisper: Word to the Wise

Vignettes IX:
September Words of Wisdom
Enrichment Topic: Shekinah Glory

Vignettes IX: September Words of Wisdom

Shekinah Glory (SG)

Introduction: The Mysteries of a Sovereign God

II Chronicles 12: 9 (AKJV) And he said to me, My grace is sufficient for you: for my strength is made perfect in weakness. Most gladly therefore will I rather glory in my infirmities, that the power of Christ may rest on me.

God is calling for a church that is free from spots and blemish. A church that is forthright, prepared and ready to fulfill His promises can now, expect Shekinah Glory. God is ready to elevate the righteous and to use a willing vessel to fulfill his purpose in the earth.

Because you have been faithful to study and practice the word of God you are next in line for a miracle. Revelations 22:5 (KJV). "And there shall be no night there; and they need no candle, neither light of the sun; for the Lord God giveth them light: and they shall reign for ever and ever." The word will bring insight and revelation. Just like a lightening bug has an internal power working in it, we the people of God should carry the power. We can enjoy the blessing and the overflow that comes from the power working inside of us. The deepest things of God are the manifestation of Shekinah Glory. When Shekinah comes you will be utterly amazed with wonder. Your eyes will bulge with wonder, your knees will weaken, your arms will flap, flail, whirl and wave. Your body will spin and twirl. If he gives you wings you will fly away and tell the news with exaltation.

Shekinah is so intense, so delightful, so distressing and yet so perfect to behold. It's a misery that births a glory, honor and dominion. The joy and pain unites to bring forth a cataclysmic Kingdom evolution that progresses us into the unusual, bizarre and extraordinary awesome places in God.

It creates a realness, a wholesomeness that sets us free from all the cares, condemnations and concerns of the earth realm. It set us on a plane to see the Supreme -the superior entities of God's kingdom. We've seen some pretty amazing things on the earth, but they will not compare to the kingdom of God. Drawing closer to God on the Earth will give us a glimpse of things to come and beauty to behold; but no comparison to the heavenly kingdom filled with the extraordinary majestic brilliance contained in the Shekinah Glory—streets made of gold, pearly gates and radiance that can never be known.

An altar and an offering are at the place of Shekinah. A special offering like no other beckons Shekinah Glory at the right time and the right season and for the right reason. Shekinah Glory is an awakening— consuming presence of God. An alertness to the character and power of God arises in man. A deep work of evolution and transformation takes place in the visual spear of those prepared and ready to advance the kingdom. A new rule of leadership and order of worship comes that makes falling to your knees petty and lacking.

A Peculiar People of God

When God gets involved in your life peculiar things start to happen – we become peculiar people. God is not predictable and He will manifest himself in ways that you could never imagine. Shekinah Glory comes in various ways in our lives at home, in the workplace and in everyday casual living. The glory of God has been known to the average man, but today the Shekinah Glory is phenomenal and above all glory that man has known or experienced.

Nice houses and cars are often thought to be the Shekinah, but it goes so far beyond the sensory awareness that the depths of our minds and intellect cannot conceive believe or achieve true Shekinah. When Shekinah comes, you won't be able to explain it with your lottery ticket, your gross annual family income or your inheritance. Shekinah is so dynamic that it happens at a speed that you can't foresee. It comes at any hour of the day and it comes when you are at your best and it comes when you are ready to throw in the towel. It ignites a worship and a praise that open up the heavens, that scatters the depths of the sea and rolls in a harvest that there is not room enough to contain.

Shekinah comes to the poor, the poor in heart, the weak, and it comes to the discouraged. Shekinah is an awakening, a stirring, a force of power that illuminates, shocks like electricity, blows like wind, burn like fire, brightens like lighting and cannot be contained. It is a quickening.

Walking with Assurance

When you know the power and glow is all God put in you, you walk in assurance. You have a confidence that says "I can walk on water". Like Peter you make a stand to do a new thing. You have overcome greater obstacles and punched out bullets and dangers seen and unseen. God lifted you up and nobody could have, except Him. When you see Jesus and his holiness, you trust that all is well–exhale.

Reaping the Harvest

You have barns bursting out, so you will build bigger houses and larger barns to contain all that God has done for you, in his magnificent glory. He has done all He promised and we must be faithful to share it with God's people. Who is worthy to partake in this wonder? We can't cast our pearls before swine because they will not value your harvest, they will waste it, burn it up and pass it on to vipers. We have to seek those with the glow and recognize the mark of Christ. Otherwise, the harvest is in vain. You cannot share your victory with people who despise you, whisper evil things about you and make mockery because they took your kindness for weakness. You cannot share the glory of God with people who are arrogant and haughty towards you. You cannot share the glory of God with people who over charge you, bark at you and leave you with "Fool on your face". Shekinah glory is not meant for men who do not believe in the principals of God. Honor, dominion and honor power remains steadfast with Shekinah Glory. It lingers like the morning dew.

The Glow of His Majesty

When Shekinah Glory comes you are strictly living in the amazement of God's favor. You have broken chain, whipped Satan and beat down his kingdom. An internal light is visible on you and shines in the darkest places. The word of God is flowing from your tongue and illuminating the environment everywhere you go. The blood of Jesus has pulled you out of the precarious places. You are walking tall and erect with a bounce that can only come from God. When the light comes, you attract the soul mate that you desire, your finances overflow and you are able to operate in amazement. Promotions and kingdom elevation manifest. Honors and achievements skyrocket. Everything you touch becomes golden. At this moment God's DNA has surpassed the world's input. The light of God is an award of virtue that no amount of money could buy. It is a present from God that says, well done, my good and faithful servant.

Shekinah Glory brings the spirit, the spirit bring healing, the healing brings eternity, eternity beckons the kingdom, the Kingdom honors the great I AM with Notorious praise to the highest God singing, 'Hallelujah, Hallelujah is the Lord God almighty who was and is and is to come.' God is faithful to bring Shekinah Glory continually when we honor and glorify His name.

Summary and Conclusion

It is important that you remain steadfast, unwavering, untiring in your commitment to share the word of God. Shekinah abides and will be sustained by your ongoing plan to serve the Lord. You should not be discouraged even when you cannot see any results from your labor. You must have a spirit of determination that keeps you going strong despite the barricades and road blocks. Be genuine and do not make any pretense. Maintain your integrity at all times. Be prepared to present the gospel to lost souls; teach redemption through the love of Jesus Christ; share the love of God everywhere you go; Let people see the power of prayer (pray for them and let them see the change); always express the importance of having faith in God. We should remain focused and not distracted by the cares of the world by being filled with praise and prayer, sharing the gospel, teaching and preaching the word of God that brings power to all who believe. The bible is your greatest spiritual tool to bring the Shekinah Glory into your life. Be a light for Jesus and His transformational powers will consume and overtake your life.

Reference: Revelations 22:5 (KJV) "And there shall be no night there; and they need no candle, neither light of the sun; for the Lord God giveth them light: and they shall reign for ever and ever."

Vignettes X:
October Words of Wisdom

Enrichment Topic: Harvest Season

Vignettes X: October Words of Wisdom

Enrichment Topic: Harvest Season

Introduction

A sacrifice of praise brings a harvest of wisdom, knowledge and understanding. It allows us to tap into the sagacity of God. We become all knowing like Him and are never taken off guard. We find ourselves saying, "They think I don't know this, but I'm already praying and prepared". The spirit of God gives us the insight, vision and the unfair advantage of having the Christian instincts to anticipate what's happening next. The more we acknowledge the harvest of God's wisdom, the more He shares and divides the spoil. When we ingratiate Him, He makes us smart and draws closer to whisper more great and mighty secrets in our hearts, minds and spirits. Luke 10:2 (NIV) "The harvest is plentiful, but the workers are few. Ask the Lord of the harvest, therefore, to send out workers into his harvest fields. The month of October is harvest season, so we should have a sense of expectation, preparing to receive the good things that God has stored away for us. As we reflect on the seeds that we have sown, we can be certain that a harvest is imminent in this fall season. If we have loved well, we will receive an abundant measure of love; If we have honored others, we can know that God has a reward of honor prepared for us; and if we have given our best, then God will release His best back to us. When we are overwhelmed with many responsibilities, the spirit of God will lead us to prioritize in such a way that everything is done at the time of inspection. Three task are due today, but the inspector only comes at 10:00 a.m. for the task that you just completed; this leaves time to complete the 1:00 p.m. task and then time for the 4:00 p.m. inspection. Early in my career, I noticed that God never allowed me to be taken by surprise, humiliated or put to shame. I did not ask for His favor, but He simply offered me His overflow of grace. When we are diligent to work with a heart of commitment and determination to complete the assignment, Jesus will never let you go astray—simply because your work is your praise. He always rebukes the devourer for your exaltation. Thanks for reading this far, you will be blessed as you continue to read these words of wisdom in the harvest season, whispered from a sovereign God. Let the work of your hands praise the Lord.

Blessings Overflowing

Being prepared for financial, social, spiritual, emotional overflow means we have a plan to disperse and execute that which God has entrusted us. Your truth, is always connected to your challenge. How well do you handle the challenge? How fearful are you of the challenge? Does the challenge break your rhythm or does it cause you to press harder? God delights in a fighter, one who won't give up and won't be defeated. When this spirit of perseverance comes to overtake you, the harvest of endurance comes to bless you.

There is a significant difference in anxiety and excitement. When we are anxious, we have an overflow of fear that God is not going to help us with the plan that we have laid out; but excitement believes that God is going to do everything in His plan, so much so that there is not room enough to contain it. We are excited and in expectation of how to store the overflow. We now contemplate what God us to do with the harvest. Why is He entrusting the harvest with me? What does He know that I will do with the Harvest that others will not do? Just look around, God has a plan just for you. I am the singer, so He will give me a studio, not only for me, but to share with others. I am the organizer, so He gives me a master plan for establishing an empire. The territory that He enlarges for me may look very different than your territory, but God knows exactly what we will do with the harvest based on the passion He placed within us. Continue to walk in your assignment and praise God for overflow.

Exceedingly great Joy, Peace and Comfort

We show our love and knowledge of God, because we are no longer moved by circumstances. If the sun doesn't shine and the wind doesn't blow, God will still provide; God is still Redeemer. A seed that I forgot about, will sprout up joy, peace and comfort. We don't know why, but today, I'm just happy. I'm very excited is what my aunt says. Nothing is new, but she has sown seeds of joy, peace and comfort to others at some unknown point in time and thus randomly, she is excited with a joy that cannot be understood nor contained. From the abundance of her heart bellows out a praise of worship that reaches to the heavens. My praise may not look like your praise, feel like your praise or sound like your praise but it breaks strongholds and catapults me into a future of blessings and honor all the same. Keep reading, writing, speaking and believing because God hears your heart and acknowledges every groan.

Gathering the Harvest

Nothing grows during harvest season because it is a time to reap, gather and collect the fruit of one's labor. Gathering the harvest allows us to reach out and receive that which was buried or non-accessible. Harvest season is time sensitive so it's important to not sleep through the harvest, or plan things that are not conducive to being in position for the harvest. Gathering cotton or grain requires having a vessel large enough to fill what is available for us. Sometimes we are not prepared for the overflow because we don't bring a bucket, sack or vehicle large enough to contain the harvest. Trucks on the highway are losing grain as they drive because the crop was greater than their space to receive. It's a sad thing when we miss the harvest altogether because we got distracted on other things, but to gather the harvest and lose 25 % on the wayside is an equally pitiful thing. Sure you have plenty, but think about the persons, who could have been blessed from the overflow.

During harvest season, we need to call our neighbors, family and friends together to enjoy the harvest. Leaving it in the field to decay, reveals our selfish nature. Once you have enough, call others to embark upon the joy of receiving a harvest. We want houses that we did not pay for, cars that we did not seek out and work for, so we must learn to give so in times of lack, the grace of God can pour out unexpected and lavish crop, where we have not sown. The gathering is the grandest point and we need to call in all willing vessels to enjoy. Just because the store sells pants with shallow pockets don't mean yours have to remain shallow. I am known to improvise because my grandmother taught me the importance of having big pockets. She wore the apron with pockets, so if any blessing came, she had somewhere to put it. Without the pockets, we are making a statement that we are not anticipating anything extra coming our way. The pockets bring encouragement and hope that something more is on the way today. As I reached into my pockets, I noticed that only a small section of the pocket has been unstitched for usage—it was only large enough to slide in a tube of lipstick. It occurred to me today that all I was anticipating going into my pockets was something as small as a tube of lipstick, so I immediately began to tear the remaining stitches open. I want enough space for everything that needs to be gathered for my pockets today. The harvest is often plentiful, but once again, we must be prepared.

Plague for the Harvest

A harvest epidemic can roll in from good seed and bad seed. If we have been impatient and unkind, a wave of unkind and bad things can roll through to chase you down and give you the blues. Likewise, if you have been patient and faithful, things will come in your favor that are done with patience and excellence to last as long as your desire remains constant. God is our father and desires to give us His best, but we may interfere with our words, deeds and dispositions. A haughty spirit is an abomination unto the Lord. Christians are expected to be humble and forgiving; not happy when others fail, not judgmental when others make wrong choices and decisions. As Christians we need to pray more and think less. We often fall into judgment because we seek to judge others. We forfeit our blessings, simply because we choose to curse the actions of others.

Prayer for the Harvest: Lord we thank you that you are a God of grace and favor. We desire to be the seed that honors others and stretch out our arms in love and comfort. Let the words of our mouth be pleasing unto you and present a fragrance of love overflowing. Help us Lord to order our steps and walk in the perfect plan that you have prepared for our success and favorable outcomes in life. Thank you for your son Jesus who gave himself in exchange for our sins. Help us to cast down imaginations and high things that dishonor who you made us to be. Live in us and let your spirit have free liberty. In Jesus name. Amen

Sowing on Good Ground

Lord we enjoy giving, but many times our love is tramped on and bounced against the walls. We intend to do good, but evil stands before us to attack and change our course. Now we understand, that not all ground is holy. Not all ground is sanctioned by you and we must be alert to retreat and move around the snares of the enemy. Everybody can't be blessed by you. Everyone does not want your $10.00 blessing, because they perceive that you gave it to intimidate them. They think your gift is an expression that they are poor and you are not. So once again, we are blind-sided, trying to do good but evil surrounds us with a double barrel and swipes over our heads like a 757 jet. We are spinning around looking for the joker and didn't know he had us surrounded. We were oblivious to the traps, the jealousy, envy and strife. What they did not know is that we gave out of our poverty and not from our abundance. They did not know that your sacrifice was for their honor, because you esteemed them greater and desired that they have no lack.

We want to remain steadfast, but there comes a time, when we have to surrender. Sometimes we must throw down the torch and let the fire fall where it may. You can't save everybody; Everybody is not your friend. Everybody is not in favor of you. There is a devil and he seeks to kill, steal and destroy.

Learning to sow on good ground is simply learning to hear and believe God. Your good deed should be received with joy and love. If there is no comfort for your good deeds, then you have sown on bad ground. If there is whispering and telling others what you did with an attitude of lewdness, the ground is tainted. Good ground will yield a harvest of peace and love. Good ground removes the tension out of the atmosphere when you enter the room. Good ground echoes back a word of encouragement to you. Good ground speaks back to your soul with warmth, patience, gentleness and kindness. Only sowing on good ground honors God. Sure we can break up stony ground, but not until the dust settles; not until we are strong enough to weather the condemnation.

Who can benefit from your harvest

A laborer understands that their work is not in vain. Something good always comes from a task conceived from a tender heart. Some labor mightily but others refuse to work, but want the same harvest. Some will take your rewards, knowing that they did not contribute in your pain. Sharing the harvest on stony ground will yield destruction and loss. Casualties occur when the crop is given to slothful workers. Crop failure occurs when others don't have the integrity and work ethics that you have to water the grain. Giving your crop to people who don't respect the assignment, takes away the honor from everyone involved. Just because you love them, doesn't mean you can share fine things with them. The bible says don't cast your pearls before swine (Matthew 7:6). "Do not give dogs that which is holy (KJV). They will trample it underfoot.

When you hire staff, you want them to have your same work drive and initiative. If they don't, they may sabotage what you have tried to accomplish. You want to duplicate yourself, because your power will be strengthened. If you are not equally yoked the pull will be too hard to finish the job. You could have done it alone, but wanted some help. However, all help is not good help. You can't take everyone with you, because some will pull you down. Take it to the master, some jobs are best done alone. The harvest is best enjoyed with those of like character. Some were not able to complete the job, but they cheered you on. Anyone who prays for you can receive from your harvest. Anyone who desires or have had your work ethics can receive from your abundance, because God want to encourage them that your labor of love is not in vain.

Summary and Conclusions

Workers are needed because God has an abundant supply of harvest to distribute. We should sow our seeds with expectations for a harvest and be prepared, having enough vessels and workers to collect the fruit of your labor. Pray for Godly wisdom to sow on good ground and avoid sowing in a field of bitterness and resentfulness. As Christians we are charged to work with a cheerful attitude and joyful disposition. Alone we can accomplish great things, but paired with more workers the reward of harvest becomes more powerful and more plentiful. Pray for strength to battle with the full armor of God. During harvest season we need no distraction and no regrets, simply preparation and readiness to receive with arms and vessels extended. Continue to sow seeds on good ground; continue to share your wealth with the poor; bless God's people and you will know continual harvest and prosperity. Reference: Luke 10:2 (NIV) "The harvest is plentiful, but the workers are few. Ask the Lord of the harvest, therefore, to send out workers into his harvest fields

Vignettes XI:
November Words of Wisdom
Enrichment Topic – Thanksgiving

Vignettes XI: November Words of Wisdom

Enrichment Topic - Thanksgiving

Introduction

During the month of November we are charged to be grateful for all of our blessings big and small. Be thankful not just for your family, but for your neighbors, co-workers, care givers, associates and friends; Be grateful for the mailman who brings good things; Be happy for the lawn service and the hairdresser, appliance repairman etc. If we are only happy for what select people do, then we are missing so many more opportunities to encourage and be encouraged by others. Matthew 5:7 states, "and if you greet only your own people, what are you doing more than others? Do not even pagans do that? Be grateful for your pastors, choir directors, youth services coordinators, day care providers. Roman 16:5 says "Greet also the church that meets at their house. Greet my dear friend Epenetus, who was the first convert to Christ in the province of Asia. Stretch your limits and show love to anyone who has remotely been good to others. No matter what their backgrounds, ethnicity or cultural experiences, people have value and we should be thankful for the good deeds that everyone contribute to life. Even prisoners and ex-cons bring value to someone and should not be taken lightly as very important people to God. Romans 16:7 Paul compels us to "Greet Andronicus and Junia, my fellow Jews who have been in prison with me. They are outstanding among the apostles and they were in Christ before I was." Too often there is a bad stigma with inmates, but Christ led by example, using some of the most feared to perform great work for his kingdom. Paul wrote the book of Thessalonians to encourage the people. We should also write words of comfort and encouragement, letting people know how important they are to us. In I Thessalonians 5:12 Paul says, "Now we ask you, brothers and sisters, to acknowledge those who work hard among you, who care for you in the Lord and who admonish you. Paul wrote the book of Romans to explain that salvation is available by receiving the word of

God, the gospel of Jesus Christ. Even the mother of Jesus worked very hard for our salvation and deserves honor and reverence. Romans 16:6 (NIV) notes, "Greet Mary, who worked very hard for us". Mary endured much whispering and judgment and sacrifice to make Jesus possible. Because she was a willing vessel, we can enjoy the blessings from her labor. Above all, we should praise God for his wonder and mighty power.

The Grace and Mercy of God

I'm often reminded to count it all joy, when confronted with test and trials, because trials work patience in me and when patience has completed it's work, nothing else will shake me because I will become an expert in patience–I will be entire, complete and wanting nothing. Colossians 3 says to put on the heart of compassion. We must do good to those who despitefully use us and say all manner of evil against us. Matthew 5: 11-12 says that we are blessed when people insult and persecute us and say all manner of evil things about us, because we have a reward coming from heaven. The grace and mercy that we render will come back to us pressed down shaken together and running over. Psalms 136: 1 (NIV) compels us to give thanks to the Lord; for He is good: for His mercy endures forever. We need His mercy every second of the day, so I urge you to praise Him, honor His for who He is and learn to trust Him in all things. Acknowledge Him and He will show you exactly how important you are to Him. His mercy is not seasonal, but it is eternal. His mercy is not based on our work, but is given out of agape love and unearned favor. In order to receive the fullness of his favor, we must stir up the gifts we have been blessed with. We are charged to love others and forgive others, as God forgives us. Now that I understand the value of forgiveness, I just smile when the enemy comes to attack, adversity because I now wonder, how is God going to get glory from this situation. Now I've learned to say thank you in the midst of a trial because I know that the righteous are never forsaken. I can fall on my knees and worship because the grace and mercy of God, covers my sins. In adversity, I know that God is greater, so

I press to cast down imagination that we tend to exalt above God. Hang in there sisters and brothers –it's just a test. In the end, we win. I John 1:9 says, "If we confess our sins, He is faithful and righteous to forgive us our sins and to cleanse us from all unrighteousness. Humility redeems us by the power of Jesus Christ, who died for the perpetuation of our sins.

How to Worship God

We should worship God with fear and trembling. Not because he is intimidating, but because He has the power to heal, deliver, save and set us free. We must worship Him in spirit and in truth. His word sustains us and His spirit give us peace. Psalms 136: 1 (NIV) reads, "O give thanks to the Lord; for He is good: for His mercy endures forever". In order to give true praise and worship, we should start with humility. Surrender your will to the will of God and allow His spirit of truth to guide and direct your daily activities. We must have a heart of forgiveness. With a humble heart we can declare the excellence of God and thanksgiving for his supreme love and we can petition our needs at His throne of grace. We can bow our heads or lifts our hands to the heavens above trusting that He will meet every need. God desires to give us the kingdom and the fullness thereof, when we approach Him with admiration. Our devotion to God is manifest in our love for our neighbors. He hears and answers prayers that seem impossible.

Benefits of Prayer, Praise and Worship

God is faithful and just to hear your supplications and have compassion for your groans. Prayer, praise and worship are beneficial because they allow us to rest and rejuvenate. Prayer gives us restoration because we pour out our burdens and place them at Jesus feet. When your plate is full, Jesus still has room. He tells us to come here all who labor and are heavy laden and I will give you rest. Worship does not require that words be spoken, just sigh, just pat your feet, or just meditate on His goodness. Even when weary utter a hand clap to let God know you recognize who He is. Some jump for joy without making a noise because they know that He lives off your praise. If we can keep Him alive without praise, we will always live to the heights of our worship and beyond. God promise to repay us for everything we do. Plant your prayers, praise and seeds of worship and prepare for a harvest that will overtake you. Whatever you are expecting, God says that your expectations will not be cut or by any means deflated. The sky is beneath the limit of what God can do to propel you into the position, place and space in life where you desire to be. Be thankful and always whisper words of praise.

Summary and Conclusions

Everything we need is in the hands of God. God is totally prepared to intercede for all of our needs and works faithfully in our praise. Doing the work before us with a humble heart and integrity breeds the love of God and the glory of God. His plan to prosper us is sovereign, all we need to do is give Him continual praise. Prayer, praise and worship defeats the enemies that come to weaken us. Falling to the earth and honoring God gives us leverage for ambush to be set by God. Your prayer is a set up for God to be miraculous. As you praise you can expect a storm to brew and separate the chaff from your harvest. Your worship will invite the peace and presence of God to manifest and calm the raging storms of life. More time with God builds us up with strength, power and endurance. We can never go wrong seeking God, because He will always come. An amazing and relentless God who cannot be distracted from meeting all of your needs and desires of your heart. This is the season of Thanksgiving. Your praise in the month of November can rescue you throughout the year.

Reference: Psalms 136: 1 (NIV) give thanks to the Lord; for He is good: for His mercy endures forever.

Vignettes XII:
Dccember Words of Wisdom
Enrichment Topic: Birthing out the Promise

Vignettes XII: December words of Wisdom

Birthing out the Promise

Introduction

This final chapter will complete the Christian's season of manifested wisdom and whispering to bring forth the new epoch of birthing out the promise of God. God promises to never leave or forsake us. He is the good shepherd who watches over His sheep. Now it is time to prove Him. This is the moment of ecstasy for Christians because at this time we can overcome with style and candor. God is granting His followers Kingdom habitats and royal living accommodations. God is healing and removing burdens and destroying yokes that have jerked Christians around for centuries. Your sincerity and truthfulness is digging up the soil and springing forth the roots of the earth to manifest the glorious new birth. Donald Lawrence and the Tri-City singers whisper in song "I heard the Spirit say, It's your time, the waiting is over, I feel blessings in the air, come into your season". God is certainly restoring the years. During the month of December, it's time to whisper that we are birthing out the promise of a Messiah who is wise and holy.

No Cross, No Crown

Each of us have daily crosses that we must bear. Every day has trouble, disaster, disappointment, confusion and strife for Christian people. Imagine after three hundred sixty five days if we, who call ourselves Christians carried all burdens and never released the annual load of burdens and cares; Imagine the weight we carry that could have been buried in the soil of forgiveness. Christians have been so loaded down with dirt that they are no earthly good. Crosses in life have value, but more than a daily measure breeds more agony than humanly necessary causing slow demise and hopelessness. Christ bore our sins therefore we can give the issues right back. Most of us like to hang on to our sins for a while and regurgitate them, relive them and become contaminated by them, but it's totally unnecessary. John 19:16-18 reminds us that Jesus was handed His cross to carry to be crucified. Jesus went out, bearing His own cross, to the Place of a Skull, which is called in Hebrew, Golgotha. There they crucified Jesus between two other men (a thief and a robber). Jesus carried this cross, a symbol of his love for us and as a token of forgiveness of our sins. If we never had a crisis or cross to bear, we would never come to the reality of knowing God. If you never escaped a car wreck that could have been fatal, you may never know His love. If you have never been on your death bed and witnessed God's miraculous healing, you would not be able to understand his power. Without a challenge, we may never solve a problem or learn to work through an issue using the wisdom of God. Imagine being in the kingdom and everything always turned out exactly like you wanted it. Imagine never having any lack in your life; you just might lose your mind if there suddenly is not enough resources to survive. We have to overcome something to become someone fit for the kingdom. If tragedy never came to visit, you could never know how God works situations out and restores us to peace. There have been times, when things were so bad, I thought I would never again experience peace and joy. But, when I let God bare my sins and strife, I counted my cares as nothing. The only explanation when nothing else makes sense is the hand of a sovereign God. Adversity bring victory, just as the rain and storms of life bring contentment. Without the water pouring down, there would be no harvest or vision of the manifested promise of God.

We all want "the third day experience", but with redemption, comes thorns, persecution and stones. No cross–no crown. The process of birth follows a long path of mysteries, thrills and pains. The steps for transition into the promises of God follows:

Conception of the Spirit

Certainly we all have heard about seed as it relates to mating and intercourse. The true purpose for intimate relationship is reproduction. God's desire is that we replenish the earth with our kind; so He requires a union that we must esteem as holy and exclusive. It typically comes with enthusiasm and excitement; likewise, your seed of prayer and expectation only takes a moment with God and should be spent with joy. The longer you engage and entreat God in prayer, the relationship becomes more powerful and healthy. Don't forget to pray about all relationships, friendships and acquaintances. Prayer is often and perhaps the last thing on ones minds prior to engaging in acts of intimacy. Many times, Christians are partnering with persons other than their spouses and married couples disregard or don't know how very importance a monogamous healthy sex life is to God. Yes, there it is, I said it, now let's deal with it. We know that God is concerned that expecting women are healthy and take prenatal vitamins with regular checkups throughout the gestational period, but we do nothing to prepare for the sensational deposit. Let's get real, we assume, "It is what it is.", but the reason most couples sneak and cheat is because they expect and build their minds up to think the intercourse and the love will be better elsewhere. The time that was spent meditating on what someone else has to offer, could be better spent praying to God to make the relationship more dynamic with your spouse, so the thought of contaminating the relationship never comes to mind. Prior to making the deposit it takes less than five minutes to pray and ask God to make the experience fruitful and allow it to honor Him. Absolutely, He is concerned because the partnership is sacred and He desires that the commitment remain constant—as His love for us is unchanging. Do you know anyone who prayed? A five minute seed allows the Holy Spirit to lift up a new standard in your life.

What you do and what you say

Now it's time to write the vision and set the plan for delivery to be sweat less and joyful. Plan for spiritual warfare, but pray for a triumphant entry into the peace and rest of God's promise. Many approach the birthing process with exhilaration and never experience birthing pains during the monthly transition. Paired with modern medicine, biblical teaching and grace, some have easy transformations. Others, are tested throughout the birthing process; the family is tested and distractions come forth day by day. Satan wants to abort the plan of God, but your faith for the seed, gestational period and triumphant entry surpasses the trickery and distractions, interruptions and diversions.

Your voice is the voice of God; your expressions in love can reach to the heavens— all God needs is just a whisper. "Hey God, remember me? I trust you and I surrender everything within me to you. Prepare me for manifestation of your promise. Give me integrity to use the life within me to honor you. Amen."

How you react as a Christian to the promise

The possibility of major life changes can be frightful and intimidating. Knowing that a foreign body lives, breathes and grows within our loins, makes us wiry, restless and weary; Excitement is mixed with apprehension. Christians wonder can they handle the responsibility of a new baby–a new season of promise. The appetite grows large as this moment and space and discomfort becomes a daily concern. Wearing this new garment is different and peculiar, it has sticky places mixed with rough edges, but we have no choice but to charge forward, regroup, gird up to recover the lost seed and unveil the promise. We are on the cutting edge of something miraculous and epic, but far beyond our ability to comprehend.

Christian Pre-Natal Care

At this season, the idea of more than enough is not deemed plausible because the true reality has not set. Christians desire a new baby of promise, during this prenatal season, but do not comprehend how the process will evolve. Maternity clothing is bought to prepare for growth with materials that stretches as the body changes. Comfort foods are bought and consumed with limited satisfaction. Migraines, sleep issues and nose bleeds happen to distract and discourage the birth. In our own minds we decide to get a piggy bank to put pennies in, we look for pacifiers and simple things to make the transition smooth. Our planning is on a small miniscule scale, but God desires to do the miraculous, while Christians' planning and execution are mediocre, at best efforts.

Monthly Examination of Progress

Checking our progress reassures that we are on course for a healthy delivery. Our level of maturity is evolving. We are growing as Christians and want everyone to know the news of the re-birth of a dead and risen Savior. The womb was virgin and now is impregnated for the world to know. Respiration and heart palpitations are strong and sonograms reveal a bright future. We are reading and studying the bible more and are excited to share the news. We are so hooked with Jesus at this juncture that we cannot contain our new revelation of who He really is and His power. We run rampant with the spirit of God that it is refreshing, comical and humbling. This is the season of prophesy where we experience dreams, visions and often a spoken word from the almighty God. We seek Him more so He comes faithfully; because He said "Ask and ye shall receive, seek me and ye shall find me, knock and the door will be open unto you". This Utopia is kingdom living and the paradise that God promised. Next, blood is drawn to determine if the DNA of Christ is healthy and on track with the promise of God.

Everybody knows that without the shedding of blood, there is no remission of sins. We need to know if the baby Christian is at risk for setback, defects or chromosomal abnormalities. This season brings life's bodily rhythms and activation of life assignments. When our sins are forgiven we are made whole and can press in for the promise.

Pressing in on the Promise

Nine months into the pregnancy, the hidden obstacles must line up and get into position to culminate the final outcomes. Some things have to move out of the way for new things to come. Last month's blessings is old wine. Now, it has to be discarded for the new improved manifestation.

Sometimes God will suggest that you give away a house, donate all your jewelry or perhaps open up a new bank account. It seems mysterious at the time, but God has a secret plan to redeem on a grandiose scale of recovery. We've outgrown our old clothing and must buy clothing to reflect our largeness in Christ. We purchase more hope, more love and give a sacrificial offering to homeless people on the street, as a measure of our surrender of praise and worship. We fall to our knees at this juncture and give in to the Holy Ghost to take over.

It's time to line up everything that is needed at the onset of breakthrough. Pressing in on the Promise occurs at this phase. Colossal outcomes require extreme sacrifices to cross the finish line of completion. Cosmic trends are breeding as we enter the phase of cohesion where the world of man and the world of God unite to become one.

Breaking the Hymen

Now it's time to utter a sacrificial praise as we scream with a burning praise of reverence, "Oh God, Oh God, Oh God", pressing in for the promise. He said He will never leave nor forsake you, so we put Him in remembrance of His word. The band of yoke is tightening and the pressure becomes more intense and seems more than we can bare. The promise spirals down in the form of flesh through the uterine walls with mucus fluids filled with tissues and membranes. The barriers began to break and the tight places that could not previously serve as points of passage, now become a thoroughfare for grand blessings to flow through the trough—the birthing canal. Just as Jesus has to make accommodations in a manger in Bethlehem, likewise we are in a tight spot whereas, all promises comes with travailing, discomfort, crib like and manger type small settings—the trough. The crib/manger of Jesus reminds us of the dark places and the trenches that Jesus had to tread to get to the place that God prepared.

If we are ever to get to the heavenly place that God has prepared for us, we like Jesus must be channeled through the tunnels of life. We must flow from the womb to the tomb, from the grave to the saved, from the earth to the heavens. Look around and find your grave, cultivate the soil and dig your way out. We have to plagiarize the life of Christ, get the wisdom of Christ. We must steal his road map to get to our final destinations. We need a borrowed tomb to step out of to serve as witnesses for new life in Christ. This is the point to praise again, "Oh God, Oh God, Oh God". The womb is your borrowed tomb in Jesus–the plan for salvation. You can step out of darkness into the marvelous life of Christ. We have to leave the earthly world of sensual pleasures and self-gratification and transcend into the heavenly world arena of service and self-denial. In order to be effective, the hymen must be broken, we have to step from mortality to immortality. The womb must be fireproof to endure the pain and suffering that goes with ripping the veil.

Jeremiah 15:18 says, "Why is my pain perpetual and my wound refuses to heal." His painful situations required the fireproof plan of God. In order to be effective in worship, we must enter into the plan of God and when patience has its perfect work, we will be complete, entire and wanting no good thing. Jeremiah went through a painful situation, but he came out purified and holy, tried and true. He was persecuted for preaching the gospel and when he tried to stop, Jeremiah experienced a burning urgency that felt as though fire was raging in the marrow of his bones. Somebody has to witness and it was his appointed season. No matter what people say or do, you have to preach and prophesy the word of God, lest it will explode inside the carcasses of your bones and break the capsule of a stony heart.

Delivery Location and Status

Now is the time to start deciding where you want to deliver the promise and who will be a part of your very important people (VIP) birthing team. Prosperity must be shared and cannot be contained alone. Many partners are needed to channel and liquidate the assets. Jesus had twelve disciples in the upper room on his birthing team, so this is a good number to achieve. Mary and Joseph were of course the overseers; All parents want to nurture their children and become a part of their success. Jesus' Ministry Birthing Team consisted of 12 Apostles of Christ: John, the beloved disciple; Phillip, the horse lover, Investigator; Matthew, the tax collector; Nathaniel aka Bartholomew, a loyal follower; Thomas, the skeptic and doubtful one, who gathered facts and asked a lot of questions, aka Didymus; Simon the Zealot, aka Thaddeus/Jude, A bible scholar/writer; Judas Iscariot, the treasurer and betrayer; Phillip, Inquired of Jesus about unity of the father and son (as evidence of his stewardship), James the Less was handpicked by Jesus; James the Great aka sons of Thunder (Fisherman); Andrew, a fisherman; Peter was the spokesman, emotional and impulsive, a leader and family man; Matthias was the chosen 12th disciple after the suicide of Judas Iscariot at the post death of Christ.

We understand from Jesus' selections that good teams need loyal supporters, a treasurer that understands money matters, but also is tested with the money. A good team need people who write, pray and ask questions, collect taxes, good spokesmen, good counselors, judges and teachers. You also need men who bait with patience and catch men for Christ. Now that your insight is fully established, it's time for birthing classes. God is your spiritual partner during your pregnancy. The promised blessings began to stir, gets restless and starts to move and show evidence of its forthcoming presentation. Key players must be in position to perform their duties at the impressive and epic event.

The Outpouring, Labor Pains and Deliverance

Dr. Luke, the Physician was not among the original apostles but he wrote the book of Luke and the book of Acts in the New Testament. Dr. Luke was a dedicated companion of Paul and stood with him during his imprisonment. We all need people in our lives that we can consult with and gain expert advice, witness and testimony. When the flood gate opens and when the outpouring comes, we are purged of all unrighteousness, we are reigning with God in the holiest of places. Right now, we need a physician like no other, we have to have Jesus right here and now—it' more urgent than any emergency we have ever experienced. The placenta cracks and fluids start leaking out, oozing out and spinning our minds that cause us to swat and push, pant and press in for the prize. It's time to recall the coaching antics and look around for the Doulas who got us to this point. If the promise does not arrive timely, you must question why and discover options for speeding up labor and delivery. The trained labor coach helps you assume the proper birthing position and provides emotional support. The husband performs this role in many cases, but sometimes faints and is missing in action, at the most critical point. Calling on the name of Jesus Christ, the greatest of all physicians is all you have left at this juncture in the birthing process. Jesus hears your cry and comes to your rescue. He delivers you from all your pain, issues and disease. He presents to you the new birth; new sons and daughters to carry his DNA of promise.

The birthing partner could make the deposit, but does not always stay in position for the outcome—the Promise. The person who sows the seeds, sometimes gets weary and miss the final moment of delivery of the blessing. God says do not be weary in well doing, for you will reap if you don't faint. Of course this is serious, true, comical, painful and sad. This is the place to stop to laugh and savor the moment. We are so close to the promise.

Walking and living in the Promise

Isaiah 53:2 (NKJV) For He shall grow up before him as a tender plant. And as a root out of dry ground. Stand fast in the liberty where with Christ has made your free and do not be entangled again with the yoke of bondage (Galatians 5:3 KJV). I would have fainted, unless I believed to see the goodness of God in the land of the living. Now we are walking in paradise, a new birth, a new season to exhale. It seems like a dream but the foundation of our history has returned to the land of plenty. We are now crucified with Christ and living in the Garden of Eden once again. A holy, lavish lifestyle where nothing is beyond our needs and desires. We are in a place of existence where there is perfect harmony; a perfect state of being in this world and the revelation of the impeccable world in life beyond the cosmos. We live on earth as human beings having a spiritual experience; but, we reign in the afterlife as spiritual beings in a heavenly province. All new experiences are powered with amazement and wonder, but cannot be compared to the glory of the coming of Jesus Christ. Some people listen to you and pretend they don't comprehend; however, they are logging it into memory. They will use it at just the right moment---to validate their goals. They want you to think your words have no value and your conversation has no impact on their lives. Nevertheless, in times of obscurity, there it is, your wise words manifesting on their tongues. You were almost convinced that they never got it— never learned. You didn't think I knew that did you? Of course I know it, and I don't mind saying it out loud. Whisper your words, write it on the tables of their hearts. The vision will come to past, though it lingers. Eternal life is the result of Christ like living. Transformation carries good and evil, but is well worth the moment of meeting Christ face to face.

Birthing Out the Promise Summary

The essence of the promise is to encourage you that God is with you and will give you knowledge and understanding to go forth with his plan and purpose. His words of wisdom will prepare you to be stronger men and women, steadfast, wise, faithful and diligent partners in every domain of life. Be ready to receive a powerful word from God to promote wisdom, favor and enrich your ear to hear from a wise and all-knowing God. A seed must endure and suffer long to manifest the promised vegetation. It presses through the soil, rises and has perpetual development and empowerment to achieve great and miraculous victories as did Christ. We have finally arrived and can live in heavenly places, feasting on the grand order of an amazing God. Celebrate the new season of perpetual manifestations of the promises of God!

Reference: Isaiah 53:2 (NKJV) For He shall grow up before him as a tender plant. And as a root out of dry ground.

Lessons to Learn

2014 Whisper: Words of Wisdom

Note* This ministry theme calendar will be a blessing to all churches who desire to strengthen ministry for women and men. It is an effective tool to motivate and prepare the ladies and men of your community for phenomenal growth in Jesus Christ. It bears repeating each year. Each month should be assigned to a different pastoral staff member using the scriptural text. It's amazing how each minister can use the scriptures in a unique and compelling way to prosper the gospel.

I urge you to share this ministry book to all church ministries worldwide and use it build up the Kingdom of God–The government of God–The authority of God.

Ministry Lessons

January- - Psalm 133:1 Behold, how good and how pleasant it is for brethren to <u>dwell together in unity.</u>

February -- I Corinthians 13:4—7 Love is patient, Love is kind

March -- <u>2 Timothy 3:16</u> All Scripture is breathed out by God and profitable for teaching, for reproof, for correction, and for training in righteousness,

April--Zach 10:1 Ask<u> the LORD for rain in the time of the latter rain.</u> The LORD will make flashing clouds; <u>He will give them showers of rain, grass in the field for everyone.</u>

May-- I Cor. 15:58 Be ye steadfast unmovable, always abiding in the works of the Lord, for as much as ye know, your labor is not in vain in the Lord.

June-- <u>Ruth 1:16—17</u> But Ruth said, "Do not urge me to leave you or to return from following you. For where you go I will go, and where you lodge I will lodge. Your people shall be my people, and your God my God. Where you die I will die, and there will I be buried. May the Lord do so to me and more also if anything but death parts me from you."

July- – II Timothy 4:7 I have fought the good fight, I have finished the race, I have kept the faith.

August-- Jeremiah 29:11 For I know the plans I have for you, declares the Lord, plans for welfare and not for evil, to give you a future and a hope.

September—Revelation 22:5 continues, "And there shall be no night there; and they need no candle, neither light of the sun; for the Lord God gives them light: and they shall reign forever and ever."

October—Luke 10:2 (NIV) ""The harvest is plentiful, but the workers are few. Ask the Lord of the harvest, therefore, to send out workers into His harvest fields.

November—Psalms 136:1 (NIV) Give thanks to the LORD, for he is good. His love endures forever.

December --Isaiah 53:2 (NKJV) 2 For He shall grow up before Him as a tender plant, And as a root out of dry ground.

Standard Order of Service

Opening Worship Song
Welcome
Statement of Mission and Vision
Communal Prayer
Song
Scriptural Inspiration
Song/Offering
Praise and Dance Worshippers
Introduction of Ministry Gift Messenger
The Message and the Invitation
Pastoral Comments and Inspirations
Pastor or Ministry Team Leader Closing
Blessing/Departure

Ministry Calendar 2017

2017 Ministry Topics

January --- Essentials for Discipleship: Starting Now

Luke 9:23 - And he said to [them] all, If any [man] will come after me, let him deny himself, and take up his cross daily, and follow me. (KJV)

February -- Experiencing God: Who is Love

John 13:35 - By this shall all [men] know that ye are my disciples, if ye have love one to another. (KJV)

March – From Bondage to freedom: Learning to win in Spiritual Warfare

Hebrews 4:12-13 For the word of God is living and powerful, and sharper than any two-edged sword, piercing even to the division of soul and spirit, and of joints and marrow, and is a discerner of the thoughts and intents of the heart. And there is no creature hidden from His sight, but all things are naked and open to the eyes of Him to whom we must give account. (NKJV)

April – Resurrection Power

Matthew 27:50-53
And when Jesus had cried out again in a loud voice, he gave up his spirit. At that moment the curtain of the temple was torn in two from top to bottom. The earth shook and the rocks split. The tombs broke open and the bodies of many holy people who had died were raised to life. They came out of the tombs, and after Jesus' resurrection they went into the holy city and appeared to many people. (NIV)

May -- Preparation for the Coming of God's Kingdom: Comparison to a Mother's Love

<u>1 Kings 2:19</u> Bathsheba therefore went unto king Solomon, to speak unto him for Adonijah. And the king rose up to meet her, and bowed himself unto her, and sat down on his throne, and caused a seat to be set for the king's mother; and she sat on his right hand. (KJV)

June - Investigation of our Destination: How committed are you?

(<u>John 1:1</u> "In the beginning was the Word").The Word of God. This is where everything in the process starts. If you're going to end up at Destination: Prosperity Overflow, you're going to have to start with the Word. (KJV)

July - Leadership: Circle of Victorious Champions

1 Peter 2:9-10 - But ye [are] a chosen generation, a royal priesthood, an holy nation, a peculiar people; that ye should show forth the praises of him who hath called you out of darkness into his marvelous light: (KJV)

August -- The Great Tribulation: Plowshares and pruning hooks

Daniel 7:25-26 [25] He will speak against the Most High and oppress his saints and try to change the set times and the laws. The saints will be handed over to him <u>for a time, times and half a time.</u>

[26] " 'But the court will sit, and his power will be taken away and completely destroyed forever. (NIV)

September - Transformation: From Caterpillar to Butterfly

I Corinthian 14:1-40 1 Follow after charity, and desire spiritual gifts, but rather that ye may prophesy. 2 For he that speaketh in an unknown tongue speaketh not unto men, but unto God: for no man understandeth him; howbeit in the spirit he speaketh mysteries. 3 But he that prophesied speaketh unto men to edification, and exhortation, and comfort. 4 He that speaketh in an unknown tongue edifieth himself; but he that prophesied edifieth the church. 5 I would that ye all spake with tongues, but rather that ye prophesied: for greater is he that prophesied than he that speaketh with tongues, except he interpret, that the church may receive edifying. 6Now, brethren, if I come unto you speaking with tongues, what shall I profit you, except I shall speak to you either by revelation, or by knowledge, or by prophesying, or by doctrine? 7And even things without life giving sound, whether pipe or harp, except they give a distinction in the sounds, how shall it be known what is piped or harped? 8For if the trumpet give an uncertain sound, who shall prepare himself to the battle? 9So likewise ye, except ye utter by the tongue words easy to be understood, how shall it be known what is spoken? for ye shall speak into the air. 10There are, it may be, so many kinds of voices in the world, and none of them is without signification … (NIV)

October – Preserving the Breed: Harvest Time Reapers

John 15:15 "You did not choose me, but I chose you and appointed you to go and bear fruit- fruit that will last. Then the Father will give you whatever you ask in my name." -NIV

2 Thessalonians 3:6 - Now we command you, brethren, in the name of our Lord Jesus Christ, that ye withdraw yourselves from every brother that walked disorderly, and not after the tradition which he received of us. KJV

November -- Growing in Grace and Favor

Colossians 4: 6 Let your speech at all times be gracious (pleasant and winsome), seasoned [as it were] with salt, [so that you may never be at a loss] to know how you ought to answer anyone [who puts a question to you]. AMP

December – The Purpose for Christmas: Finding Bethlehem

Luke 2:8-20
[8] And there were shepherds living out in the fields nearby, keeping watch over their flocks at night.

[9] An angel of the Lord appeared to them, and the glory of the Lord shone around them, and they were terrified.

[10] But the angel said to them, "Do not be afraid. I bring you good news of great joy that will be for all the people.

[11] Today in the town of David a Savior has been born to you; he is Christ the Lord.

[12] This will be a sign to you: You will find a baby wrapped in cloths and lying in a manger."

[13] Suddenly a great company of the heavenly host appeared with the angel, praising God and saying,

[14] "Glory to God in the highest, and on earth peace to men on whom his favor rests."

[15] When the angels had left them and gone into heaven, the shepherds said to one another, "Let's go to Bethlehem and see this thing that has happened, which the Lord has told us about."

[16] So they hurried off and found Mary and Joseph, and the baby, who was lying in the manger. [17] When they had seen him, they spread the word concerning what had been told them about this child, [18] and all

who heard it were amazed at what the shepherds said to them. [19] But Mary treasured up all these things and pondered them in her heart. [20] The shepherds returned, glorifying and praising God for all the things they had heard and seen, which were just as they had been told. (NIV)

Strategic Plan for Salvation

- Recognize and admit that you are a sinner

- Repent by having a renewal of mind, heart and spirit

- Verbally confess and believe in your heat that Jesus was raised from the dead by the power of God almighty.

- Commit to being baptized in water and by the spirit of Jesus Christ.

- Commit to studying the word and making Jesus Christ first in your life.

The lifestyle of a Disciple is to read the bible daily; pray constantly, worship every day; study your bible and fellowship with others; attend church regularly; serve others as they need, share your resources with others financially and share your special gifts.

THE END

Key Terms and Definitions

Grace = God's unmerited favor; When we have access to good things that we don't deserve. King Cyrus was given unmerited favor and empowerment from God.

Mercy = The compassion and forbearance of God, whereas we are spared a punishment that we did deserve.

Whisper = Whisper is a soft expression of a message of power. Speech using one's breath, without using one's vocal cords typically for the sake of privacy. A rustle or murmur. A confidential tone of voice, a low voice, undertone.

Wise = An astute, prudent usage of rational statements understood with soundness, quality of having knowledge and using it for good. Advisable, supple enough for information to flow through and retain for proper usage. Scholarship, sophistication, learner of insights.

Words = Vocal output with expressed meaning. An audible display of intellect, verses, statements.

Websites

http://www.bibletools.org/index.cfm/fuseaction/Bible.show/sVerseID/26679/eVerseID/26679/RTD/Clarke/version/nasbe

http://www.merriam-webster.com/dictionary/per

http://www.whatchristianswanttoknow.com/20-inspirational-bible-verses-about-grace/#ixzz3Frr9XNgH

About the Author

 Dr. Sharon Denise Malone Waddle, is a native of (Limestone County) Athens, Alabama. She was born September 14, 1959 to Mr. Ollie Malone and Mrs. Imogene (Lucas) Malone. Her sons Benjamin Waddle and Martez Waddle (God sent) both inspire and encourage her to excel in writing. Benjamin has served as content editor for this book and is a great task master. Dr. Waddle is a graduate of Tanner High School ; She completed her Bachelor and Masters' degrees in Clinical Psychology from Alabama A & M University; and she completed a doctoral degree from Capella University in Industrial Organizational Psychology. Dr. Waddle uses her writing skills and poetry as ministry tools to advance the Kingdom of God.

Dr. Waddle is a member of Calvary Assembly of God in Tanner, AL. She aspires to impact the world by whispering a word to the wise from a Sovereign God.

Printed in the United States
By Bookmasters